Library of
Davidson College

The Peal of Bells

The Peal of Bells

BY

Robert Lynd

Essay Index Reprint Series

BOOKS FOR LIBRARIES PRESS
FREEPORT, NEW YORK

First Published 1925
Reprinted 1969

STANDARD BOOK NUMBER:
8369-1226-8

LIBRARY OF CONGRESS CATALOG CARD NUMBER:
78-90660

PRINTED IN THE UNITED STATES OF AMERICA

TO
Arthur St. John Adcock

CONTENTS

Chapter		Page
I.	The Peal of Bells	1
II.	The Mouse: A Problem	9
III.	The Street Preacher	18
IV.	The Sixth of December	25
V.	Seaside	33
VI.	Continued	41
VII.	Hotel	49
VIII.	A Good Hiding	58
IX.	Horses	67
X.	In Defence of Patent Medicines	76
XI.	Looking for an Ancestor	84
XII.	Heat	92
XIII.	Experiences of a Voter	99
XIV.	On Being Cruel	107
XV.	Puzzles	115
XVI.	The Christmas Present	124
XVII.	School	131
XVIII.	On Going to Scotland	139
XIX.	The Collar	147

Contents

Chapter		Page
XX.	This Body	156
XXI.	Change	164
XXII.	Worry	172
XXIII.	In the Casino	181
XXIV.	The Quarrel	191
XXV.	Laziness: Written in Winter	199
XXVI.	Solitude	207
XXVII.	Farewell to Tobacco	216

The Peal of Bells

I. *The Peal of Bells*

"Surely I shall not spend my whole life with my own total disapprobation."—Dr. Johnson *on his 72nd Birthday.*

IT is a new year, and I have begun a new life. This, I think, is better than merely talking about it. But it is more difficult and brings one just as little credit. No one, indeed, seems to observe the signs of the new life except the man who is leading it. I once had a friend who told his wife that he was beginning a new life, and who went with her to a New Year's Eve party at which he thought he was being particularly abstemious, while she thought he was denying himself nothing. The next morning he complained of a headache. "Of course, you have a headache," she told him, and added: "I thought you said you were going to begin a new life." "Much good there is in beginning a new life," he retorted bitterly, "when you don't even notice it. Last night *was* the beginning of the new life!" He, I suppose, remembered chiefly the things he had refused at the party, while she remembered chiefly the things he had taken. There is always this personal element in our judgments of ourselves and of each other. We cannot go about, unfortunately, telling everybody about the temptations we have resisted.

The Peal of Bells

As a result, people judge us exclusively by the temptations to which we yield. This is very hard on those of us who are unusually susceptible to temptation and who frequently succumb out of sheer inability to go on resisting for ever.

Knowing myself intimately, I am able to take a more sympathetic view of myself than other people can be expected to take, and I forgive myself for shortcomings that in anybody else would distress me. It is a very unhealthy frame of mind to get into to be always reproaching oneself for one's peccadilloes. I am sure the most cheerful people are those who confine their censures almost entirely to the lapses of their neighbours. This is also, I hold, the more modest attitude. Like other people, I desire a better world, but I have the wit to realize that I alone can do very little to improve things, while other people could improve the globe out of recognition in seven days, if only they would conquer their evil instincts. They are the human race; I am a helpless individual, an onlooker. It would be mere conceit to regard my own faults as being half so serious in their consequences as theirs. Hence I feel an honest glow of pleasure when I see other people behaving well, and I am melancholy when I see, or even hear of, other people behaving badly. I often long to direct them with good advice, and refrain only because I know that friendship itself will not stand the strain of very much good advice for very long. And so, while I am inwardly aching to preach to my errant

The Peal of Bells

fellow-creatures, I find myself talking to them instead about diet, diseases, cinemas, Bernard Shaw, and the day on which I backed three winning horses at Ascot. I doubt, indeed, if I have ever warned even an intimate friend against one of his minor faults. I doubt if any of my friends know that I know their faults. In spite of the pain that our friends' faults cause us, we keep up a fantastic pretence of blindness in order that we may remain tolerable to each other. That is why we have to talk behind people's backs. There is no other chance of talking freely. Then Truth comes out of her well, smiling and without a blush. How good it is to learn the worst about our friends and acquaintances from her impartial lips! "A shrew"—"Drinks, doesn't he?"—"He's as mean as the devil"—"He and his wife quarrel in public so"—"The foulest bore in London"—"Always looks as if he had spilled soup down his waistcoat"—"Ruining himself gambling"—"He's got the most appalling swelled head"—"He's such a coward. Always runs away." These are the sort of things it is much better to say *about* a man or a woman than to say to their faces. There is such a thing as tact, which reminds us, for example, that, if we wish to tell the truth about a conceited man, it is better to wait until he has gone out of the room. He will not resent it then. He is so conceited that he will not even guess that we are saying how conceited he is. Some people would condemn this as scandalmongering. But surely it is

The Peal of Bells

better to tell the truth behind people's backs than never to tell it at all.

Besides, if we are to abolish this form of veracity, how are we going to preserve our moral standards? It is by listening to gossip about our friends that we learn to distinguish between right and wrong, and, as we see their reputations being torn more and more rapturously to pieces, they serve as a kind of awful warning to us, like the penitents confessing their sins at a revival meeting. And they are more fortunate than the penitents, for they do not have to confess their sins; we confess them for them. That grave, rather sad-looking little man—you would never guess what his vice was till someone told you, when he had gone, that he had written an "Ode on the Intimations of Insobriety," and that his wife did not guess his secret till one night after he returned home from a party she found him folding up a bath towel and carefully putting it away in a drawer under the impression that it was his evening suit. From tales such as these we learn what sins to avoid and the importance of being careful, but not too careful. And if the sin of which we are told does not happen to be one of our own favourite sins, to join in condemning it is noble practice in moral enthusiasm. Thus, the miser is a moral enthusiast as he condemns the spendthrift, and the spendthrift as he condemns the miser. The drunkard becomes a moral enthusiast as he tells the truth about the amorist, and the amorist as he tells the truth about

The Peal of Bells

the sot. The hypocrite, the sluggard, the glutton, the flatterer of the people, the slum landlord, the sweating employer, the harsh mistress, the lazy workman are all capable of such moral enthusiasm; and moral enthusiasm is not a thing with which we should part lightly.

Even so, I find it more difficult, as I get older, to confine my moral enthusiasm to the lives of other people, and I grow egotistically concerned about the life I myself am leading. I should not have believed you if you had told me twenty years ago that at my present age I should not have settled into more admirable and virtuous ways. The faults of a man who had reached or passed middle age used to surprise me when I was a boy, and if I saw in him signs of vanity or fear or greed or ill-temper, I disliked them as something unnatural. It seemed to me extraordinarily easy for a middle-aged man to be virtuous, and, indeed, I could hardly imagine what middle-aged men could find to do except behave well. I saw that a number of them abstained from doing so, but in their self-indulgences they seemed to me to be as defiant of common sense as white blackbirds. As I grew from boyhood to youth, I came to like many of these self-indulgent elders, but I thought of them chiefly as "rum coves," eccentrics, "old sports," and never as normal human beings who had arrived at years of discretion. When I came to read Horace in class, I learned that it was by no means easy even for a middle-aged man to be virtuous, but I never-

The Peal of Bells

theless remained sure that virtue was more temptingly within reach at the age of forty than at sixteen. And I knew in my bones, though not without sorrow, that Horace was right when he affirmed that there was a stage in life at which it was time for a man to bid good-bye to folly. As I sat under the stern eye of a master, and heard the Latin being translated into schoolboy English, I felt wave after wave of emotion sweeping over me—a wave of self-pity followed by a wave of intense resolve to play the man at some future date—at those curfew lines with which the second Epistle of the second Book of Epistles ends:

> Vivere si recte nescis, decede peritis.
> Lusisti satis, edisti satis atque bibisti;
> Tempus abire tibi est, ne potum largius aequo
> Rideat et pulset lasciva decentius aetas.

Even to-day, when I can no longer read Latin, and have to guess what "decede peritis" means, the lines continually haunt my memory and bring back those feelings of luxurious regret with which a boy many years ago used, in anticipation, to bid farewell to Epicurus and subscribe himself a Stoic. Alas, despite all this, I find myself as I grow older approaching much more nearly to the likeness of one of those "rum coves" I used to laugh at than to the graver portrait of the Stoic I admired.

Yet somewhere in me, I feel sure, a Stoic is buried and awaiting resurrection. "Ye're a young Stoic,

The Peal of Bells

Master Y.; ye're a regular Trojan," my nurse used to say to me, when she gave me some base medicine in a teaspoonful of raspberry jam and I took it without wincing. I did not know at the time what the words meant, and I don't think that she knew either, but I was pleased by her flattery, which she lavished on me on all occasions of discomfort or danger. If she took me to the dentist's or put a lava-hot poultice on my chest, she always began and ended with: "Ye're a young Stoic, Master Y.; ye're a regular Trojan"; and, though it was not true, it made me feel a better and happier boy. Looking backward, I see in it an unfulfilled prophecy which I surely ought to have set about fulfilling some time ago, and I feel a better and happier man. What if now at last I should adopt the advice of Horace to himself —should listen even to the counsellor in my own breast—and should say to myself gently:

> "Lusisti satis, edisti satis atque bibisti:
> Tempus abire tibi est,"

and rise from the table of pleasure and leave the sweet dishes of folly to younger mouths? There is something attractive to me in the prospect. The bare and frugal board of the Stoics has its own charm. There is no pleasure to surpass that of deliberation. Philosophers aver that the chains that bind me are so fragile that they will break at a touch, and indeed that, at a mere wish, I can sever them one by one—indolence, self-indulgence, envy,

The Peal of Bells

fear and folly—and escape. How delightful to achieve a godlike indifference to the things that one knows do not really matter and that do matter to one so much! How else is it possible to become serene—which is the visible grace of wisdom? "A man," my doctor tells me, "is either a fool or a physician at forty," and it is also true, I fancy, that at that age a man is either a fool or a philosopher. O miserable choice between the rival pleasures of folly and philosophy! I have tried for a long time to combine them by enjoying the pleasures of folly in practice to-day and the pleasures of philosophy in anticipation to-morrow. Even that, however, becomes a jangling and uneasy compromise with advancing years, and I grow more and more convinced that some time or other, sooner or later—perhaps this very year—the grand break with folly must be made. In facing this fact, I feel that I have taken the first step into a new life, and, so far, the New Year seems to me to have begun excellently well. "Lusisti satis." True. . . . Good night, folly! Good morning, virtue!

II. *The Mouse: A Problem*

IT is an engaging problem in ethics whether, if you have been lent a cottage, you have the right to feed the mice. There will for most people be only one answer to the question. Your first duty, they will tell you, is to the man who has been good enough to lend you his house, and you must do nothing that would damage it or even that would annoy him if he knew about it. On the other hand, it is reasonable to argue that the feelings of a mouse that is present are more to be considered than the feelings of a host who is absent. Besides, he need never know anything about it. He may be surprised on his return to find mice running up the clock, mice cantering up and down at the side of the fire-place, mice playing on the floor under the table, mice in his jam cupboard, mice nibbling the corners of the books on the lower shelves, mice, in fact, behaving as if the house were a vast restaurant for themselves and a crèche for their children. But, as he is a good man, he will put all this down to accident, and will never suspect that the people to whom he lent the cottage could have done anything so disgraceful as actually to scatter food on the floor and invite the mice of the neighbourhood to make themselves at home.

The Peal of Bells

I can write on the question without bias, because during the week-end I was the guest of the people who were feeding the mice, and at the same time I was sleeping under the roof of the man during whose absence the mice were being fed contrary to his interests and contrary, I am sure, to his wishes. Besides, I liked the people who were feeding the mice, though I could not altogether approve of their conduct. The mouse-hole was a large orifice in the varnished floor near the hearthstone, and, when the lamp was lit, the smaller of two girls went for a biscuit, broke it into small pieces, and placed these carefully in a ring round the hole. Then she sat down and, in perfect stillness, watched the mice till bed-time. I asked her if it would disturb the mice for the rest of us to talk, but she said that the mice did not mind, that they were accustomed to it, and, indeed, were quite tame. A few minutes later I had just got to the point of what I thought was a rather amusing story when she interrupted with a vibrant, excited whisper, "Look at the mouse." Strange, when there is a mouse in the room, it is impossible either to tell or to listen to a story. I do not like being interrupted, but I found myself staring with the others at the little cave in the floor from which the head of a mouse had projected, like a jack-in-the-box, and was looking round at the world with its nervous, beady eyes. It apparently came to the conclusion that we did not look very dangerous—that, indeed, we were merely a number of harmless luna-

The Mouse: A Problem

tics—and hoisting itself, head and shoulders, out of the hole, it seized a piece of biscuit and ducked back out of sight with it again. There was a chorus of "The little darling!" "Isn't it perfectly sweet?" "Oh, the angel!" "Did you ever see such a darling little pet?"—for so it is that angels and darlings in human form express themselves at sight of an animal they really like. Still, thinking of the unfortunate man who owned the cottage, I could not help reminding them that their attitude to the mouse was one of mistaken kindness. I pointed out to them that, when the owner of the house returned, he would be able to catch the mice all the more easily on account of their tameness, and that to teach them to trust human beings was merely to lure them to their deaths. Nor would death be less bitter to them, I suggested, when they told themselves that it was due to the treachery of women and children. At this, the lady all but broke down, and I thought for the moment I had persuaded her that the most humane thing she could do was to try to frighten out of its wits every mouse that put its head through the floor. "Oh, yes, indeed!" she cried, wringing her hands, as she pictured the doom of the mice at the return of the proprietor; "it's *quite* true." But the elder of the children demurred. "*I* think it's silly," she said. "The mice will be caught anyway, whatever we do, poor little things. All the more need for us to give them a good time while they're alive." "That, also, is quite true," said the lady,

The Peal of Bells

brightening up. "And now," she went on, turning to me, "let's have the rest of the story." It is by no means easy to take up the thread of an anecdote that has been interrupted just as one has got to the point. "Well," I said, "you remember how Godfrey was left with the insurance policy." "I'm afraid I've forgotten," she apologized. "The argument about the mice has driven everything else out of my mind. Do begin all over again from the beginning." I hate having to repeat a story, but I obeyed, and was just reaching the point again, and smiling with satisfaction at the thought of the effect it would produce, when the small girl at the hearth once more called our attention with a hoarse, excited whisper: "Look, it's coming out again!" Once more all heads turned on necks and all eyes were concentrated on the little cave in the floor. This time the mouse did not merely thrust its head and shoulders out of the hole. It shot itself out bodily, and scampered along the floor behind the coal-scuttle. "That's the father," said the romantic one of the small girls; and again there were enthusiastic cries of "The darling!" "The angel!" and "Dear little thing!" I made no attempt to recover my anecdote, but I am afraid its double disappearance prejudiced me against the humane treatment of mice. I looked on them as my rivals—as my horribly successful rivals. Everybody, I told myself, was far more interested in mice than in me.

Yet I have always liked people who were kind to

The Mouse: A Problem

mice. I once knew a man whose bedroom was infested with mice. He bought a trap and set it, and during the night was awakened by the struggles of a mouse that had been caught in it. He immediately got up and released the mouse, and, next day, threw the trap into the dust-bin. Nor would he ever use a mouse-trap again. And I loved him for this. I also feel tenderly towards two maiden ladies of my acquaintance who are on such good terms with the mice in their flat that if ever they go away for a holiday, they leave a little heap of meal on the floor "for the mice." The mouse, it seems to me, is a creature that we should all like, if it were not such a nuisance. Children like sweetmeats made in the shape of mice. They like a toy mouse in a cage. There is in the shape and the bright eyes of the little creature something that appeals to our affection. It is a natural pet, if it would behave like a pet. It is impossible to make war on it without twinges of conscience. There is in Coleridge's correspondence a charming letter to Cottle, in which he declares that he is threatened by famine on account of mice, but that he cannot bring himself to set a mouse-trap. He says that to bait a trap is as much as to say to the mouse, "Come and have a piece of cheese," and that, when it accepts the invitation, to do it to death is a betrayal of the laws of hospitality. Certainly, when you come to think of it, no Borgia ever treated a guest more dishonourably. The only honourable way to make war on mice, it seems to me, is not to

The Peal of Bells

deceive them with any pretence of friendship, as who should say, "This is Liberty Hall. Here's cheese for you," but to keep a cat and let the mice come out of their holes at their peril. Most people, however, would like even cats to be more humane. They hate to see a cat actually killing a mouse. It is an unequal battle, and the cat seems to enjoy it. Such things are, no doubt, necessary. But, if they must go on, they should at least go on out of sight. We may not mind conniving at the murder of a mouse, but we object to being made spectators of it and, as it were, participators. Man, after all, is a sportsman. Or a hypocrite. Or both.

As for wasps, that is another matter. Who minds killing a wasp? The only people I ever knew who minded killing a wasp were people who were frightened that the wasp would sting them before they had killed it, or that its friends would come and sting them after they had killed it. At least, those were the only people of the kind I had known till I went down into the country for the week-end. There I found a lady and two children behaving almost, though not quite, as tenderly towards wasps as towards mice. If a wasp all but drowned himself in the marmalade at breakfast, they would exclaim, "The little darling!" and one of them would carefully take him out on the point of a fruit-knife and carry him over to the window-sill to dry his wings in the sun, poor thing! Heaven knows I have no special antipathy to wasps. I am not afraid of

The Mouse: A Problem

them; I move backwards at their approach merely as a precaution against accidents. Even so, I see no sense in encouraging them to such a point that one cannot eat a meal without a veritable Pleiades of wasps dancing round one's head with a noise like the noise of an orchestra of muted violins playing distressingly out of tune. It is not that I duck more nervously than other people. In fact, I often hope that other people do not notice that I am ducking at all. But it cannot be good to eat one's meals in an atmosphere in which, all the time, one wishes to duck. It is also rather disturbing to the flow of the gastric juices to be constantly wondering, while chewing one's food, whether one is looking nervous and what the children are thinking. "There's one on your collar," one of the children cries delightedly. "Don't move." Not for a ten-pound note would I so much as breathe, as she gently encourages it to fly with a spoon. "Sweet little thing!" she comments, as it sails off into the air to join its fellow-fiddlers. Drawing a breath of relief at being rid of it, I say: "They seem quite tame." "Wasps," says the little girl, airily, "would never hurt anybody, if people didn't hurt them." I should like to be able to believe it, but I have heard the same thing about dogs and about human beings.

There was, I afterwards found, a wasps' nest in one of the apple-trees in the orchard. It was in a hole in a rotten branch, and, when I went out to see it, I observed the wasps from it burying their bodies

The Peal of Bells

down to the waist in the not too numerous apples of the man who had lent the cottage. Here, too, it seemed to me, was a situation in which one's duty to the man who owned the house was at least as important as one's duty to the lower animals. The only valid excuse for leaving the nest was that no one knew how to destroy it. I did—at least, I had heard that it could be done with paraffin oil—but, as I was afraid I might be asked to do it myself and that some of the wasps might come out in a mood of annoyance while I was pouring the oil on their nest, I said nothing about it. Even if I had, however, I doubt if I should have been allowed to interfere with them. The wasps were "little angels," "little darlings," and so forth, and must not be touched. And I must say, the wasps appeared grateful, and, though they always seemed to be going to sting one, they never actually did so. Indeed, I was becoming quite accustomed to them at meals, when some people came to tea, and a lady, who took the conventional view of wasps, kept striking them away from her face with her hand as she talked. "Do you mind them?" our hostess asked her innocently. "The sting of a wasp," said the lady, as if taken aback by such a question, "is exceedingly painful." And she struck at another of them. The worst of it was, she always waved her hand in such a way as to strike the wasps over towards me. "Here," thought I to myself, feeling miserable, "she is infuriating Olive's tame wasps, practically pointing

The Mouse: A Problem

me out to them." And, as they buzzed round my head, I could hear that their note had altered and had gone a semitone higher . . .

Since I returned from the week-end, I have been seriously considering two questions in my mind. One is, whether it is possible to be kind to mice without being cruel to your host. The other is, whether it is possible to be kind to wasps without being cruel to your guests. There is something to be said for the old-fashioned attitude to certain of the wild creatures.

III. *The Street Preacher*

TWO street preachers, of whom the world at large never heard, have died within a few days of each other. They were both called "Sammy." One was called Sammy Sloan, and the other was called Sammy Thompson. When they died, however, the obituary notices in the local papers were headed: "Death of Mr. Samuel Sloan" and "Death of Mr. Samuel Thompson." You could not have told from the obituaries that two of the oddest figures of their time had gone to heaven, and yet it is for the oddity of their speech, appearance, and passion that they will be remembered by most people in their native city. Of Sammy Sloan I knew little. I heard him preach once, indeed, but it was only occasionally that he came out of the mission halls and spoke at the street corners. But I shall always remember his laugh, which was frequent and infectious as he recalled the sins of his past, and compared the clothes he used to wear in his drunken days with the clothes he and his family could afford now that his soul was saved. He was taller than the crowd, dark, lean, with a streaming brown moustache that you would say had been specially created to be dipped into pints of porter; and his description of the temptations he suffered before

The Street Preacher

he was converted was given in the spirit of a divine knockabout comedy. He described how the furniture went, the clothes went, and the very boots went—"up the spout"—in order to satisfy his wild craving for drink. "Anything for a pint," he said with a laugh that suggested that he still saw the fun as well as the sin of it. Not that he failed to paint the miseries of a drunkard's home—the ill-furnished rooms, the wife lacking clothes and food, the children with holes in their boots. And, indeed, if he laughed, it was chiefly with delight at the comedy of the salvation of so bad a character as himself. He described, with his eyes shining, the new furniture in the house, his wife's new bonnet, his children's new boots, all the direct consequences of a drunkard's coming to Jesus. "Look at this coat," he shouted, his face radiant with joy, as he caught the collar of the jacket he was wearing. "A fairly respectable coat, don't you think? How much do you think it cost? I won't tell you; it might make you jealous. But do you think I would be able to afford a respectable coat like this if I hadn't given my heart to Jesus? No, friends, only for Jesus, this coat might now be lying on a shelf in Kerrigan's pawnshop, and I might be sitting in a cell in the police barracks, repenting with a sore head." He took such a manifest and childish pleasure in the wonders of his destiny that you could not help warming to him, and it is said that he persuaded thousands of people to change both their faith and

The Peal of Bells

their lives. His laughter, indeed, which was the first thing passing strangers would notice, must have been only the public advertisement of an imagination that was at once passionate and poetical. Did he not say that for him, when he went out of his house on the morning of his conversion, the streets of his native city shouted for joy, and the islands at the mouth of the harbour clapped their hands?

Sammy Thompson, though he may have succeeded, like Sammy Sloan, in making other people laugh, never laughed in public himself. "There's no laughing in hell, boys," he would bark hoarsely, turning round to reprove some irreverent youths who had come up to listen at one of his street meetings. And, when Sammy Thompson reproved you, you stopped laughing. He was generally believed to be an ex-convict, and was a middle-sized man of heavy build with the fierce bull-dog face of a prizefighter. He had close-cropped hair and a mouth that, at the end of every sentence, shut like a rat-trap. He did most of his preaching from the stone steps of a public building, and, pacing up and down at the top of the steps, he would roar in a husky voice to an audience of half a dozen as though he were addressing thousands. Further on, other speakers were addressing from the steps immense and excited audiences—were abusing each other with opprobrious names such as "Long Tom the Bubble-burster," and were rousing the passions of the crowd for a raid on a little church into which a

The Street Preacher

clergyman had been papistical enough to introduce *Hymns Ancient and Modern*. Sammy Thompson was so eager to save his fellow-mortals from hell, however, that he cared for few of the things about which men fight. He was a simple man with only one idea in his head, and, as he looked this way and that with knitted brows, you would have said that even this one idea was too much for him. He made long pauses between sentence and sentence, as he thought out some new way of making clear to a lounger against a lamp-post the fact that God loved him, and had sent His Son down to earth to die for him. If the lounger against the lamp-post doubted that God cared for him, Sammy reminded him that similar miracles of love were happening every day. "Listen," he said, jutting out his chin. "Maybe you're married. Maybe you're not. I am. I've often told you from these steps about my Mary Ann. She's the best wife ever a man had, and you might wonder what a woman the like of her could see in a man the like of me. Look at me," he cried fiercely, holding out his arms so that we might get a full view of him. "That's the man that Mary Ann loves," he declared after a moment's pause, and nodded in agreement with himself after he had said it. Then the blood streamed into his face and he raised his fist to heaven and shouted: "I'm the coorsest-looking character in Bloomfield, but—she *loves* me!" He walked a step or two, and, with another nod, added quietly and quickly, "Mind that, now!"

The Peal of Bells

It was the great merit of Sammy that he always gave a personal expression to the gospel he preached, and that he was not content to repeat texts and *clichés*. He even invented his own proverbs. I heard him one Sunday afternoon saying: "God never gives a man half a shirt. He covers his whole back." But it was his weekly autobiography, rather than his epigrams, that proved him an artist and no mere dealer in pious formulas. One day, when he was preaching against hypocrisy, he suddenly paused as if he had remembered some horrible thing. "Oh, God," he groaned, throwing up his arms in despair, "here I am denouncing highpocrisy, and me wearing a dickey and pretending it's a white shirt!" And he dragged the offending dickey out from under his waistcoat for the scorn of the onlookers. On the whole, Sammy's view of life was a severe one. He thought of the Devil as an enemy whose temptations encircle us like the air we breathe. He fought the Devil even in his business, which was that of a carrier with a small cart. He was one day engaged in removing furniture, when the man for whom he was doing the job brought out some porter bottles to put on the cart. Sammy looked at the bottles with horror and waved to the man to take them away again. "This cart," he said, "belongs to Jesus Christ and Sammy Thompson, and there's no room on it for the Devil's truck."

Sammy, indeed, had abundance of that simple faith which is justly said to be more than Norman

The Street Preacher

blood. For him everything in life, down to the most trivial detail, was consecrated either to Christ or the Devil. He made it the test of everything on earth, whether it belonged to Christ. And he usually suspected that it did not. He once began to hold up as a terrible warning a young man whom he had seen going out of the next-door house swinging a cane and smoking a cigar. But even here Sammy paused to remind his audience of the universal test. After giving a picture of the young man such as suggested that he was going airily on his way to the Devil, he bent forward with flushed face and narrowed eyes and in words like hammer-blows bellowed: "I don't mind a young man swinging a cane, *if* the cane belongs to Jesus. I don't mind a young man smoking a big cigar, *if* the cigar belongs to Jesus." But it is questionable whether Sammy really gave the young man the benefit of the doubt. He did not believe in smoking, and I remember hearing him relate, as a thing almost too horrible to mention, how he had seen a young fellow and a girl walking along the road, both of them smoking cigarettes. He had gone straight up to them and warned the girl that she was letting the young man put hell-fire into her mouth, and it was one of the successes of a good man's life when she threw the half-finished cigarette on to the road. "There's no smoking in hell," he said grimly, "not cigarettes, anyway." I could sympathize with the girl's nervousness, for it was by no means easy not to quail be-

The Peal of Bells

fore Sammy when he looked at you as if he saw the Devil in your soul and longed for a tussle with him. I was rather alarmed myself one night when Sammy came into the church in which I was sitting and stared round at me like a boxer about to strike because another boy who was with me persisted in carrying on a conversation during the singing. I did not quite realize the danger I was in, however, till I heard that after the service Sammy had gone round to see the preacher and had said to him, "The Devil was in the church to-night, and I was sorely tempted to go over and throw him out." Even so, now that he is dead, I think of him not as a tyrannous, but as a friendly figure. None that ever heard him could help being moved by the news that he was dead and that his funeral procession was to meet at those cold steps that had been the scene of his triumphs and that there over his coffin other mouths less competent would try, with how small a reward, to bring heaven and hell before the imaginations of mortal men who think more of publichouses than of Paradise. Sammy, whatever you may think of him, knew at least that this is a wicked world, and he did his best to mend it. And he failed. And that may or may not be the end of the story.

IV. *The Sixth of December*

THE child to-day is expected to take an interest in current events, and even to know what is happening in politics. Hence, at the approach of a General Election, which was to take place on the 6th of December, it was natural that the schoolmistress should write down on the blackboard the question: "What is happening on the 6th of December?" The children wrote down their answers, some guessing right, some guessing wrong, and one rather optimistically guessing "Christmas." But the perfect answer was given by a serious little boy who wrote: "Granny's chauffeur's birthday." It is delightful to know that he was given full marks for this, for, after all, what child can truthfully say that the General Election is of half so much importance to it as such an event as "Granny's chauffeur's birthday"? It is true that if granny were standing for Parliament, even granny's chauffeur's birthday might fade into comparative insignificance. But an election which involves the fate merely of Mr. Baldwin or Mr. MacDonald or Mr. Asquith—how can we expect it to take precedence in splendour of interest above the birthday of someone actually connected with the family? Those who have forgotten how glorious an event is a birth-

The Peal of Bells

day may look down on a child so indifferent to public events. But most of us can remember a time when a birthday—especially if it was one's own—brightened the world as if a second sun had risen. Do you not recall how your heart beat faster every time the blessed thought, "This is my birthday," romped through your brain? If a master scolded you at school, you felt: "Ah, if he knew it was my birthday, he wouldn't talk like that!" At home you were (in your own eyes) a young king whose word was law. The world was kind, laying presents at your feet. You beamed good nature as the cake was cut—your cake—and lavished in double slices on those less important members of the family who had no birthday—at least, on that date. Heavens! the lighted dining-room was like a new star, specially created for your pleasure. I am not sure that a birthday was not even more wonderful than Christmas. After all, Christmas was a sort of universal birthday, and, though it was exceedingly good, it did not make you feel almost as if you were personally responsible for it. The 20th of April—how I used to love the look of it, even in the *Mother Siegel's Syrup Almanac* that dropped once a year through the letter-box! It was always to that date I turned first in order to see what the weather was going to be like. I do not know whether I ever believed those weather forecasts, but I was depressed if I read that the 20th of April would be "rainy, with cold wind." Selfish nursling though I was,

The Sixth of December

however, I was not entirely without interest in the weather on the birthdays of my sisters and brother. After I had read about my own—and it would be putting an impossible strain on human nature to ask that I should have done it sooner—I turned the pages and faithfully looked up the birthdays of all the other members of the family. Even to-day, I confess—no, hang it, it's hardly decent to confess this—when anybody hands me a birthday book, I would first of all look up the 20th of April and read the motto under it, if I were sure that I could do so without being observed. If the motto says something like:

> Self-reverence, self-knowledge, self-control,
> These three alone lead on to sovereign power,

I am elated. If, on the other hand, it says something like:

> Yon Cassius has a lean and hungry look,

I feel as melancholy as if a fortune-teller had found something wrong with my line of life. It is the same with those astrological birthday books. If one of them says: "A man born on this date will have a hard struggle at the beginning, but success and riches are in store for him in middle life, and he will have a healthy and prosperous old age. He is sure to be popular, especially with the fair sex. He will be as brave as a lion, but is unlikely to be confronted with any serious dangers. If he has a fault, it is that he is too ardent and generous, and he must be on the watch against false friends who care only for his wealth"—if, I say, I find something of that kind written in a birthday-book about people born on the 20th of April, I am nearly as happy as if it were all true. It has been a source of lifelong humiliation to me that, in those almanacs that give great events for every day of the year, I never could discover that any great event happened on mine. I do not care to share a birthday with Napoleon III, and that, I think, is the best that any of the calendars can do for me. I suspect that Shakespeare was born on April 20th. But the scholars, who are, however, only guessing, persist in putting the date about three days later.

A birthday, indeed, gives you a kind of new patria, and you like to have as your fellow-daymen persons of whom you can feel proud. Englishmen are proud to have Shakespeare for their countryman. St. John's College men are happier in their college because Wordsworth once studied, or avoided study, there. Human beings have a passion for the best company, and they have a fellow-clubman's interest in anyone who was born on the same day as themselves and would boast of him if they could. Thus there is nothing duller than to share one's birthday with a battle—perhaps some small battle in Afghanistan of which one has never heard. If I had my

The Sixth of December

way, I should exclude all battles save a few world-shaking victories from the calendars.

Decent children, however, as I have said, are not mere egotists in their feelings about birthdays. There is an overflow of interest in the subject sufficient to cover the birthdays of nearly everybody they know. They can read the birthday-book of one of their friends with as eager a curiosity as though it were *Treasure Island*. They regard it as a stroke of fine comedy if they find that someone was born on the 29th of February, and, indeed, as they reckon ages by birthdays, some of them would count a man of forty, who had been born on that date, as only ten years old. They feel more fortunate, too, than the child who was born on the 25th of December. There may be a certain vanity in having been born on Christmas Day, but it cuts down the likelihood of presents by half—at least, it cuts down by half the number of those days of delight on which presents are given. But the only really terrible thing that could be imagined happening to a child in these matters would be to have no birthday at all. There are, I believe, children dwelling on the earth whose birthday nobody has ever remembered, and who cannot, alas! remember it for themselves. To think of them is to conjure up an image of as lightless a world as Moses ever found himself in. According to all honest children, everybody must have a birthday and everybody must have an age, and they cannot understand the reluctance of some of their

The Peal of Bells

elders to answer them directly in regard to both. They know the ages of their friends better than the dates and the wives of the kings of England. They are incredulous if their own ages have been forgotten by one of their parents. They believe that even God must have an age. "How old is God, daddy?" said a very small child, after having succeeded in finding out the ages of her father and her mother. Her father tried to explain that God was old in a different way—that, indeed, he was eternal. "Is He a hundred years old?" asked the child. "Oh, yes," she was told, "He's more than a hundred—far more." "Oh," said the little girl, "if He's more than a hundred, you needn't tell me, because I can only count up to a hundred." It was surely a fortunate thought of the Christians to give God a birthday. Those who speak ill of Christmas Day should remember that, even if God had not had a birthday, it would have been necessary to invent one for Him for the sake of the nursery.

The child's answer about granny's chauffeur's birthday, however, seems to me to be evidence, not only of the universal interest of the young in birthdays, but of their generous inquisitiveness into the lives of everybody with whom they are brought even casually into contact. If you go into the garden, you will find two little girls in close conversation with the grey-bearded gardener, and, if you listen, you will hear a fire of questions as persistent as a barrister's in court. He is asked his birthday and

The Sixth of December

his age, and then follow: "What is your favourite flower?" "What pudding do you like best?" "What kind of fish do you like best?" "What is your favourite colour?" "What is your favourite vegetable?" "Which do you like best—beef or mutton or chicken?" Could a saint be more sympathetically inquisitive? The gardener is obviously touched, for he answers the questions gently one by one. It is true that he gets out of answering about his age by a trick. He says that he is over seven and under seventy. He confesses, however, that his favourite flower is a red geranium, his favourite pudding a boiled treacle pudding, his favourite fish a nice cold steak, his favourite colour magenta, his favourite vegetable sometimes boiled turnips and sometimes fried onions, and that he likes boiled mutton with caper sauce better than either beef or chicken. It is a proof of the saintliness of the children that their countenances do not betray the growing horror they feel at his answers. But, when they run into the house for lunch, they are bursting with the news: "Mammy, do you know what Mr. Griggs says his favourite flower is? A red geranium!" "He says his favourite pudding is boiled treacle pudding." "He says he likes boiled mutton with caper sauce better than chicken." Go into the yard later in the afternoon, and you will find the same two children putting the same questions to the elderly red-whiskered builder who is half-way up a ladder doing something to a broken spout. "What is your favourite flower?" comes from one of the small upturned faces. "A glory dizzhen rose," comes back, with a grin, from the cropped red whiskers. He is altogether a man of superior tastes, for he likes broad beans, and plum pudding, and salmon, and the blue of a swallow's back, and prefers chicken to either beef or mutton. Mr. Griggs had provided the children with low comedy. The builder's conversation is in comparison a fairy-tale, and they are ecstatic. I wonder how granny's chauffeur would come out of a similar test. Now that we know his birthday, I for one should like to know what is his favourite flower, what is his favourite pudding, and which he likes best—beef or mutton or chicken? I shall be disappointed if he says his favourite vegetable is parsnips, but I don't think granny's chauffeur could be so wicked.

V. *Seaside*

WAVES of butterflies seem to rise from the sands and to pour tremulously over the sandhills. It is impossible to tell where they come from. They might be born of the sand, or the sea, or the sun for all the eye can tell. Never before have I seen white butterflies, foes of cabbages and of gardeners, in such numbers. They flow inwards like a tide. They stagger over the hills like armed men. I do not know how long this goes on, for, ten minutes after I have begun to notice it, lunch is ready at the hotel, and I have not the courage to be late for lunch. The sandhills, however, are never free from butterflies. Brown, white, and dappled red, they wander all day among these barren heights and hollows, like creatures of the first world that rose and became dry above the waters. Bees, too, are here, black and red, getting a living among the blue flowers of the sea-holly, and the great drifts of sand are marked with the footprints of birds and rabbits and creatures as small as mice. How grasses find a place in which to root themselves, or the yellow hawkweed, or the dove's-foot geranium, in so vast and parched a soil is a mystery; but the life of the land begins thus early at the edge of the sea, and there are banks of rest-

The Peal of Bells

harrow and of heartsease and fields of evening primroses—a thousand lamps at a time towards twilight—within a stone's throw of the sea. A lark rises and sings—a song that seems different from that of the English lark—as one sits on the crest of a dune and looks out over the waste of the sea or back over the waste of the sandhills and breathes the peaceful air of these butterfly days.

Down below on the *plage* hundreds of tents have descended on the sands like a horde of striped butterflies. Men, women and children move among them like pretty insects. They wear red and green and white and yellow, and, for a mile or more, they are all exquisitely busy doing nothing. The most industrious of them are flying kites like large yellow and black birds. Little boys are doing this as a pastime. Elderly men are doing it with more intensity as a pursuit. They let out the cord gingerly from the reel, and, if the kite does not soar heavenward, they tug against it and restore it to grace. Even on a holiday one remains a moralist and notes that neither kite nor man can rise high save by opposition. The little boy's kite that is left to its own devices on a loose string dives to the ground. It is the kite of the strong man, engaged with him in a perpetual tug-of-war, that hangs in the air halfway to the sun, an afternoon's miracle. The kite-flyer, however, is solitary in his pleasures. He may have a companion, but his companion is only a spectator, not a fellow-player. Even if he flies his

Seaside

kite in competition with a rival, he has no need of a rival. He is perfectly happy to be alone and looking up at the sky and the bird that he has sent soaring almost out of sight and whose very wings quiver like those of a hovering hawk. The more sociable mortals on the strand are playing with balls of one size or another. They are playing tennis without a tennis court, cricket without a cricket ground, croquet without a croquet lawn, football without a football field, golf without golf links, rounders—every ball game that you have heard of. They play idly in the costumes of idlers. They do not care whether they hit or miss. The ball is a mere excuse for doing nothing restlessly. Few men and women, and fewer boys and girls, are content to remain still. They must move like the butterflies. They must circulate like the bees. Thus I think there is very little danger in the heresies of those philosophers who have praised indolence. It is not possible for any man but a philosopher to be indolent and to be happy. And the philosopher's is a mere indolence of body that permits a livelier circulation of the fancy. These striped tents are not the wigwams of indolence but an encampment of new activities. Even doctors tell us that the chief danger of holidays is not that we may do too little during them but that we may do too much. I myself have, alas, no bat, but I have a walking-stick, and, with a red india-rubber ball and with two children's spades for a wicket, a game of cricket can be extemporized as satisfactorily as though one were playing against Yorkshire. Not that I ever dare to play such a game on the open sands. But, in the secret places of the hills, with no one but the angels looking, have I not struck like Mead or Woolley? I doubt, indeed, whether, if Mead or Woolley had to play cricket with a soft ball and a walking-stick, they would not find their averages considerably lowered. I am sure, however, they would rather play cricket with a walking-stick and a soft ball than not play it at all. Almost any game with almost any ball is a good game. The round ball is the symbol of perfection, and man is never so care-free as when in pursuit of it. He masters it as he would master this globe of waters. He strikes it, and he is playing with a star. He cannot play marbles without repeating in little the pattern of this universe of spheres. It is possible that a mystic might even make something out of the little hesitating ball in the casino.

Not that there are not other noble games besides ball-games being played on the *plage*. Who could be more excited than the young shrimpers pushing their nets along the bottoms of the pools? It is remarkable what a difference there is between shrimping as a game and shrimping for a living. What more melancholy figures ever invaded the sea than the women dressed in black and with black shawls over their heads, who wade up to their waists at low tide, pushing their great nets before them,

Seaside

their heads bobbing up and down, like the heads of tired horses, at every step? They march like a silent procession of mourners. They are bowed like labourers in the fields. If they catch a shrimp, they do not pause and call to each other with excited cries. Even a large crab brings no shout to their lips or light of triumph to their eyes. On and on they move, backwards and forwards, silent sisters of the waters, scouring the floors of the sea for creatures that will not fetch a penny a dozen. Yet children will do all this for pleasure, and a shrimp remains to them a wonder of ocean. It is, I suppose, the money taint that destroys the pleasures of shrimping, fishing, digging, and all those amusements of childhood that are afterwards turned into a trade. On the sands a thousand gallant diggers are at work with no thought of money. They build castles and fortified towns, dig wells and channels. They labour with spade and bucket, and no child needs to "ca' canny." Here and there even an elderly father joins in the task. One man, fat of face, fluent of moustache, and with the grey of fifty years in his hair, is turning out pies from a bucket for the amusement of a child just learning to walk. He holds out a pie on a spade with the air of a waiter setting the riches of a restaurant before a guest. "Alors, monsieur, vous êtes servis," he says, bowing to the child, "—avec du frangipan." The child totters a yard forward and with one slap sweeps the pie into ruin. He laughs and looks up at his father for commendation. The father sparkles with pride over such a deed of such a prodigy, and sets to work filling the bucket with another delicacy doomed to the same fate. Happy is the father whose child finds his attempts to amuse it amusing! Further along the sands another grey-haired father is less fortunate. Poor man, he is evidently longing for a little exercise, and his infant will not advance above a yard in five minutes. Every time it sees a shell it pauses, stoops down, balancing itself carefully, and picks it up, and then, balancing itself carefully again, utters an inarticulate grunt and holds the shell out for his admiration. He had probably been admiring shells for hours when I passed him, for he looked very much exhausted. He had even begun to try to distract the child's attention from the shells by dancing round it in his bare feet and making faces. He was an odd and pathetic figure, as his wildest fandangoes and most tortured grimaces failed to win from the child even the benevolence of a momentary stare. It evidently regarded all this leaping and leering as none of its business, and balanced itself over another shell with admirable gravity. Two, I think, is the serious age. At this age it is a rare child that is not company too sober for a parent in whom age has run to skittishness.

All day long, amid all these parents, babies, diggers, kite-flyers, and players at ball, a constant stream of human beings flows across the sand, some in

Seaside

bathing costumes, some carefully hidden in wraps and towels till they reach the edge of the sea. One lady motors down to the front in a bathing costume and trips across the sand under a seven-coloured parasol, with a maid and a can of water waiting to wash the sand off when she returns out of the sea to the bathing box. Along the edge of the sea *sauveteurs* either stand or walk slowly up and down, a red tassel at the top of their blue tam-o'-shanters, their white trousers rolled up to the knee, a life-line rolled up and hanging near their waist, and a long straight trumpet in the hands of each. The bathers congregate in groups in the shallow water. If one of them ventures out a little further than the rest, a trumpet springs to a *sauveteur's* lips, and such a tooting begins that even a drowned man could hardly help looking round to see what is the matter. There are apparently all sorts of dangers here—holes, channels, and undertow; and the *sauveteurs* keep up a blare of music, especially on a day of wind and waves, that chills an ordinary bather's marrow. Even little boys on sand-castles are not allowed on such a day to remain on their castles till they have been washed down by the tide. Long before this happens two *sauveteurs* are blowing their hardest and gesticulating to the boys to come back to safety. Were they members of Captain Ahab's crew, looking out, harpoon in hand, for Moby Dick to rise out of the waters, they could not scrutinize the sea with more desperate anxiety. They are sterner than schoolmasters even with the oldest of us. They terrify us with their gestures and deafen us with their trumpets, so that all that some of us can do is to stand in a foot and a half of water and stare at them spellbound. I do not know if there is any penalty for disobedience except getting drowned, but here no man—not even if he be lawless as an Englishman—dare disobey. There are those who would despise bathing under such a tutelage of trumpeters. But I find that it suits me exactly. There is something very comfortable about sitting down in two feet of water. It is warmer than the water further out, and it is a great deal safer. After all, the chief virtue of a bathe is that it makes one wet, and this fortunately can be achieved without attempting to swim the Channel. I am not one of those who cannot enjoy the feeling of salt water without knowing that, if I sink, I shall go down thirty or forty feet. To roll about in the breaking waves, like a jelly-fish after a storm, is, believe me, no mean pleasure. Never willingly shall I cause a bead of anxious perspiration to break out on a *sauveteur's* brow. I am content to wallow in the shallows of these sunny waters under the kites and the blue sky. Thus can I loll in the ocean as lazily as on the sandhills, and not even the blasts of trumpets, addressed to wilder and more daring spirits, can perturb me out of my peace.

VI. *Continued*

IN England I have certainly often joined in the laugh against people who live in long suburban avenues in little red brick houses with names like "Chatsworth," "Sandringham," and "Portofino." That a public-house should have a name has to me, as to others, seemed to be a delightful thing; but that a private house should have a name, when it was in a street and might have had a number, has seemed scarcely less offensive than a war profiteer's signet ring or the loud tie of the son of a too *nouveau riche*. I remember how profoundly alarmed—nay, shocked—I felt when, on taking up my home in a small villa, I found the painters about to renew on the gate-posts the traditional name of the place, "Belgrave House." Yet, had I been a publican, I should have felt no scruples about hanging out a sign from my house bearing some such name as "The Swan's Neck" or "The Chained Bull" or "The Prodigal's Return." Is it foolish oversensitiveness that makes this difference between public-houses and private ones? Or may it not be that the publicans of England have preserved a finer tradition in the naming of their houses than the burgesses? The burgess is too often tempted to let his snobbishness, rather than his fancy, roam in the choice of an address. The name of his house expresses his self-importance instead of his playfulness. He would rather live in a house called "Hatfield" than in a house called "The Blue Posts" or "The Green Dragon." I do not mean that a majority of suburban houses have names so palatial as "Hatfield." But there have, since the middle of last century, been a sufficiently large minority that have fallen victims to pretentiousness to make the fastidious town-dweller feel that there is safety in numbers. Even so, I think the reaction against the naming of houses has gone too far. It is natural to give names to anything we like, or even to anything that we don't like very much but have to live with. Do not the soldiers during a war give names to the very guns—"Long Tom" and "Big Bertha" and "Archie"? Give a child a ball, and within twenty-four hours it will have named it "Pobble" or "Pamby." A man of genius buys a motor-car and calls it "Gladys." I know a man who calls his anthracite stove "Lucy." Sir James Barrie created something of a sensation by calling the stomach "Little Mary," but, long before Sir James had written a play, men who really loved their stomachs had given them personal names. I knew one man who called that part of his body "Alice," and who, when he was thirsty, would look at his watch and say, "It's time Alice had a bottle of stout." He used to describe the long walks he and Alice had together, chiefly along country roads that led from inn to inn,

Continued

and the pleasant time they had in "The Goat" and "The White Horse," and such places. He was the most faithful of lovers, and he and Alice were never seen apart till the day of their death, which their friends described as a case of double suicide, but for which the doctor, too tender-hearted to speak ill of the dead, put the blame on alcohol. Then there are dandies who have names for each of their ties, and who, when they rise in the morning, say to themselves, "Shall I wear George to-day? Or Bobo? Or La Sorcière Verte? I think, perhaps"—raising the blind and looking out at the weather—"La Sorcière Verte." The truth is, the naming of things, apart from houses, has become in recent times a positive craze. I know one household in which the passion for giving everything a name goes to such absurd lengths that, when listening to the conversation, you never know whether it is about a child or a cat or a hot-water bottle or a clergyman or a fountain pen or a motor-car or the bathroom geyser or the gardener. We have all but recovered from the epidemic of initials that swept over the world during the Great War, but we still live under a plague of names and nicknames for which even the psycho-analysts, exorcising in the names of the three great deities, Psyche, Libido and Complex, have so far been unable to discover a remedy.

Here, in a seaside resort in France, I confess, I resign my prejudice against names, and find them entirely charming. There is a little terrace of three

The Peal of Bells

wooden houses in a street that runs at right angles to the sea. The first house is called "Pif." The second is called "Paf." The third is called "Pouf." I cannot pass these houses without feeling as happy as though I were listening to a gay tune. "This Gallic levity!" I say to myself, smiling. "How perfectly charming! How light as a feather compared to the more laden, lumbering, 'What-ho-she-bumps' humour of the more solvent islanders! What *gaieté de cœur!*" I go on becoming more French at every step. "What"—relapsing into memories of the 'nineties—*"joie de vivre!"* It is obvious that if the names of houses can give the passer-by such a run of delightful sensations as this—can so introduce him to the spirit of a foreign country that he feels all but a naturalized citizen of it—the more people who give names to their houses the better. Even "Petit Robert" charms me, though it sounds less like the name of a house than of a cheese. As for the semi-detached villas, one of which is called "Romulus" and the other "Remus," I like them second only to "Pif" and "Paf" and "Pouf." And yet I should not care for any of these houses if they were only "number 3" or "127," or, as on the Finchley Road, "999." They have no attractions but their names. I have seen a "Piedmont" in England that could beat any of them. "Rose de Mai" is different. Not only should I like to live—for a summer month—in a villa with such a name, but I covet the house itself as I covet health or money.

Continued

This daffodil-coloured villa with its deep blue window-frames—the architect seems to have put into it his dream of holiday—of sunshine and seascape and all the things that could make a man happy if it were possible for him to be happy without ceasing to be a man. Then one steps across the *digue* and comes to the bathing-boxes, and most of these, like the houses, seem to have names—possibly the names of the houses with which they are connected. One of them, I notice, is in a very rickety condition. It is tilted over on its side on a great sand-heap, as though it had been blown down in a recent storm, and is, I fancy, no longer habitable. It is called "L'Entente Cordiale."

On the whole, however, I think the chief charm of a holiday in this part of France has to do not with the houses, or even with the names of the houses, but with the crabs. There are shallow pools in the league-long sands near where the wreck of a stranded warship is every day washed into greater ruin by the tides, and they are fuller of crabs than any I have ever known. Not ordinary crabs that you can, but shouldn't, eat, though there are plenty of ordinary crabs, too. What monsters these are, by the way! What liars! What cannibals! Their backs covered with barnacles, they lie against a stone like a piece of the stone, hoping to escape detection, or, with a coat of green seaweed on their shells, they sink eye-deep in the sand and seem in their stillness to be a part of the bottom of the pool. Take a walking-stick, however, and prise one of them out of the sand, and I shall be astonished if you do not find that he has a smaller crab in his claws, waiting till you are gone to make a meal of him. For some reason or other, it revolts me to see an animal eating another animal of the same kind. I can forgive a man for eating a cow, or a bird for eating a fly, or a cat for eating—well, not a bird, but a fish. But dog does not eat dog, and man, though the most ferocious of animals, does not usually eat man if he can get anything else. Brought up in the old-fashioned school that regards these things as being of a piece with the Ten Commandments, I confess I was appalled to find crab eating crab in almost every depression of the shore. Again and again I fought with a large crab for a little crab's life. I did my best not to hurt even the large crab, but the vicious way in which he bit with his pincers at my walking-stick would have roused a hotter-tempered man to reprisals. Even as he fought with his pincers, however, he did not forget to hold his victim all the faster in his multitude of thin legs. This lay, poor thing, curled up as if already beyond hope; and it was only when the monster, rolling over in the water, loosened a limb for a moment that the other would begin to kick and show itself alive. At last, when it was set free, it would scuttle underground till the sand was over its eyes, while the greater beast made sideways rushes at it and had to be driven away till it had disappeared into safety. Dear creatures of

Continued

the seaside, if you behave like this, what can you expect of human beings, who live in slums and in suburbs? I trust that being eaten is not so painful as it seems to the imagination, but, believe me, this is a dangerous example to give to beings so impressionable as men and women. We, too, prey upon each other, but not to this limit. It is only the sheep and the ox and the chicken that have to fear the voracity of our appetites. Can you, like us, not establish farms of subject beasts and learn to dine outside the degrees of consanguinity? And yet my heart bleeds for you, poor, goggling-eyed monsters, that you should have to go without your dinner merely because you meet an animal who was brought up on the Pentateuch. Did I do right, did I do wrong, in intervening in these family orgies? Did my knightly services to the little crabs seem to you mere robbery and pillage? If one of you, maddened by the pangs of hunger, had bitten me in the leg, I should have had to admit that it was but human. All the romances about ogres and distressed maidens have been written from the point of view of the distressed maidens. No one has given a thought to the ogre's point of view, except a few modern novelists, and they are not good novelists. Compare with these monsters the little hermit crabs that live in sea-shells. How pretty it is to see a company of tiny sea-shells, blue and pink and white, walking with tiny crabs under them about the edges of a pool! Some of the crabs are no larger than a pea: few of them are larger than a bean. How a creature with such an array of limb and armature can make its home in a small periwinkle shell is one of the mysteries of nature. Take up one of the shells in your hand, and the crab retires into it as into a kennel. Leave it back in the water, and it is out again wearing its shell like a hat as it runs and shambles over the uneven floor of the pool. I am not prepared to say that these delightful and amusing creatures do not eat one another even as other crabs do. I can go no farther than to say that, on the occasion on which I saw one of them approaching another in a suspicious manner, the smaller crab did not wait till I had time to settle the question by ocular evidence. Hence, I shall do my best to go on thinking well of hermit crabs. They are such toys—grotesques that might be fitted into a fairy's thimble—as they traffic hither and thither with their borrowed houses on their backs, while the spotted jelly-fishes float above them in their long draperies and indolence.

VII. *Hotel*

IF ever you go to St. Gaufre-sur-Mer for a holiday, do not, I advise you, stay at the Hôtel Jamais Encore. "That's a very fashionable place," my friends said in surprise, when they heard that it was to St. Gaufre that I was going. "It won't be," I assured them, "after I get there." I did not realize, however, that any shock I could give St. Gaufre was nothing to the shock St. Gaufre was going to give me. True, it was raining when I arrived—raining so solidly that, as I drove from the station, it was less like travelling by motor-car than by submarine. The Hôtel Jamais Encore did not look its best in the rain. Grey, cement-fronted and in a side street, it looked humble, mournful and deserted, as though the last guest and even the last servant had fled from it, as *I* wished to fly. There was no face at any window; there was no one in the doorway or in the hall to greet us; everywhere was a dead silence. Then out of a dark passage came a nervous-looking little man in spectacles, who shook hands with us as effusively as if we had been the first human beings he had seen for years. "Ah, well," we said to each other, laughing almost too boisterously as we were left alone in our rooms upstairs, "what does an hotel matter at the seaside? We shall

The Peal of Bells

be out all day. We shall merely sleep and eat here." Thus we spoke in the simplicity of our hearts.

Heavens knows, when I went to bed that night I was ready enough to sleep. But there are certain kinds of insects to which I have such an antipathy that I have always disliked even mentioning their names. When I was a boy I scarcely believed in their existence save in the jokes of those who found it easier to be vulgar than to be funny. It was not till I had come to London and taken a top back room in Vauxhall Bridge Road at six shillings a week that ineluctable monsters came out of the darkness and taught me that men had not jested on such a theme without cause. That was a long time ago, however, and even then it did not reconcile me to the existence of the names of these insects in human speech. They seemed to me the most indecent of all words—unfit to be mentioned in the presence of women or in public-houses. You will realize, then, how profoundly disturbed I must have been when in the middle of the night I awoke in the Hôtel Jamais Encore, switched on the light, jumped out of bed, seized the French pocket-dictionary with a view to an explanation with the landlord in the morning, and, muttering horrid blasphemies, looked up the French for a ——. No, I cannot write it down. But, as I looked in the glass and saw a mountain-range of bites, at once unnaturally white and unnaturally red, stretching round my neck under the left jaw and ear, I made use of words far more reprehensible than the

Hotel

name of an insect that, after all, must live, or at least acts on that supposition. On returning to the bedside, I confess I was surprised to see a little creature of which I did not even know the name, scuttling out of the light. It was a little round red spider-shaped insect of the sort that used to appear among the carrots—or was it the turnips?—at Steyning. Over the scene that ensued let me draw a veil. There was a tell-tale bloodstain where he died. But the blood, I felt, was my own, and his only by conveyance. At the same time, I lay down again with a sense of relief. This insect, I told myself, was probably an agricultural insect that did not really belong to the hotel, but had come into the railway carriage when those peasants got in at a wayside station. I could not quite forget my sufferings, however, and, every few minutes during the night, I would find myself striking a series of hurried blows first on my neck, then on my knee and finally and resoundingly on my chest in pursuit of a little red spider with soft, swift, silent feet. "Fool," I reproached myself the next moment, "you are imagining red spiders." For, indeed, when once you begin to think about spiders or ——s in the dark, the imagination becomes uncontrollable. In the morning, finding that no one but myself had been attacked, I decided that the spider must certainly have come from the peasants on the train and to say nothing about it to the landlord. Even though I spent a great portion of the next two nights in delivering

The Peal of Bells

convulsive blows at all parts of my body, and though my arms and neck were swelling almost out of recognition, I assured myself that it was merely the poison working itself out. I felt certain that if the same thing were going on as a regular feature of the life of the hotel, marks of disfigurement would be visible on the other guests. I cursed those peasants as peasants had never been cursed before. On the fourth night, however, a fiercer assault than usual roused me from my bed with the roar of a wounded lion, and, switching on the light, I beheld not only another red spider but, three inches ahead of him, my old enemy of the Vauxhall Bridge Road. Here, too, as in the Greek plays, the scene of bloodshed that followed the recognition must be left to the imagination. It is enough to say that, when all was over, I took up the pocket-dictionary again to refresh my memory as to the French for —— and also for "leave the hotel immediately." (I always say "laisser" when one ought to say "quitter.") I thought of one fine sentence to thunder at the landlord. "Monsieur," I said, glaring at him—he wasn't there, of course, for I was in my bedroom and it was three o'clock in the morning—"Monsieur, votre maison est une punaiserie." I cannot, however, be melodramatic in daylight, or even, indeed, ordinarily brave; and I was glad of it afterwards. The landlord was much more frightened than I was, accepted the facts without question, swore that it had never happened before, that it would never happen again, that he would give me a new bed, that he would have the floors scoured with paraffin. We parted on the best of terms—quite sentimentally, indeed. It turned out, if the chambermaid's story was true, that he had put himself to great expense in order to give me an all but regal bed—that he had gone so far as to buy a second-hand wooden bed, a second-hand mattress, and (I suspect) second-hand blankets specially in my honour. The chambermaid, as she looked at the second-hand bedstead, spoke of it as "le grand lit" with profound respect. She saw my point of view, however, about the insects. "Peu agréable," she admitted, nodding her head gravely. I thought this was understating the case. . . . That, then, was the end of the wooden bedstead. Never till the following night had I realized what a perfectly beautiful thing is a good, new, cheap, modern iron bedstead that has no links with the past.

As for the food at the hotel, it used, after the first week, to amuse me to watch the face of a newly-arrived guest as course followed course in a positive, comparative and superlative of evil. His expression would change with the courses—from incredulity to dismay, from dismay to repugnance, from repugnance to wrath, and from wrath to despair. Those of us who had been there for some time already, and who had become resigned to our fate, took a malicious pleasure in noting how new-comer after new-comer passed in the course of a day or two from hot rebellion to limp submissiveness. Every new-comer in turn, I think, went out after dinner on the night of his arrival to look for a room in one of the other hotels. But the other hotels were all full, and he was far from home, and, besides, it was only for a few weeks. He, too, in a day or two, was finding the joy of his life in the observation of new guests at their first meals in the hotel. I confess my heart was wrung when a young man and woman on their honeymoon arrived. They looked so happy, sitting at their little table, till the soup arrived. It was the soup that always brought to the face of the new arrival the expression that meant: "It isn't true. It isn't true. It simply can't be true." It was a soup that had many names and two colours, but it was always, save by an accident, the same soup. In its simplest form it was called "Soupe verte," which was greasy water mingled apparently with grass-clippings from the town lawn-mower. Sometimes the grass-clippings would become more abundant, and it would become "Soupe au cresson." A few potatoes would be added, and it would be called "Potage something or other." It would change its colour to brown, and it would be "Potage something else." Sometimes it had too much salt, sometimes it had too little, but never had it any other flavour save of this and of the grease. I had often tasted bad soup, but never soup so badly made from such simple materials. Apart from grease and salt, there was nothing in it but meanness. Even the bread that you got with it tasted as if it had been baked

Hotel

in the meanest bakery in the town. "The worst bread I have tasted since the war," an elderly Englishman muttered wrathfully on the night of his arrival. In three days, alas, he had become a common chuckler, like the rest of us, as some new victim came in with a hopeful, hungry look that, at sight of the meal set before him, rapidly changed to the agonized expression that you find on a Greek tragic mask.

Someone suggested that the landlord's wife still did her cookery according to the instructions in some such book as *Simple Recipes for Wartime,* or *Making the Best of Our Offals,* or *The Fungus and Its Place in the Menu.* Sometimes, it is true, we got fish. If we were very lucky it was dabs. If we were moderately lucky it was the bones of a whiting. On ordinary days, however, it was fish that in the menu was given a name for which my little dictionary contained no English translation. It was not even cod or hake. I fancy it was the kind of fish that in the cheaper London restaurants is simply called "fish." But even this was better than the offals that were the only alternative. There was, for instance, the underdone kidney of an animal that I did not recognize. It was better to eat it; if you did not, it would be chopped up on the next day and put into an omelette. Then there were *rognons sautés au vin blanc,* which sounded attractive. The *vin blanc* was a lie, and I never felt quite sure about the *rognons.* They were little hard squares of dark

The Peal of Bells

brown boot-leather, each of which had to be swallowed whole like a pill or not at all. These, too, or what was left of them, would reappear the next day in the disguise of an omelette. In my admiration of the way in which from one inedible dish another dish still more inedible was made, I found myself gazing one day at the omelette and thinking of the old hymn: "God works in a mysterious way, His wonders to perform." I was frequently driven back to the poets, indeed, in order to be able to express my feelings adequately. And the drink was as bad as the food. One has often heard bad claret compared to red ink, but this was red ink mixed with the juice of unripe black currants. When I tasted the first glass, I laid it down, and, as soon as I was able to speak, I declared roundly:

> "Good God, I'd rather be
> A pagan suckled in a creed outworn."

But these memories are too painful even to continue to write down. The pork out of season, the red mutton, the impenetrable *biftek*, the *veau* that might be tolerable and might not, all eaten amid the buzz of great, fat, black flies against which you waved knife and napkin in vain, and this usually followed by a dish of unripe peaches or unripe grapes or of overripe plums or greengages—night after night we went through them like a bitter comedy, and afterwards fled first to the coffee and brandy in some café and then to the gambling-rooms, bright halls of

Hotel

oblivion. The odd thing about it all is that, so far as I know, we all had a thoroughly enjoyable holiday. I should not go there again, but I shall always remember the time I spent there with pleasure. My one regret is that I did not bring away a menu with me. I should have liked to preserve a permanent record of those luncheons and dinners at which brave men and women turned despair into comedy and their miseries into a jest.

VIII. *A Good Hiding*

THE more I thought over it when I got home, the more warmly I told myself: "I should like to have given him a good hiding." There are times when it is borne in on me that the only thing worth being is a man of muscle—a boxer or a wrestler or a Rugby footballer, or even just a strong man like Sandow. I should not much care which. Simply to be able to hold somebody up in the air by the scruff of the neck and make him feel what a worm, a toad, an object of loathing to all decent human beings he is—if I could do that, I should not wish to strike him. Still, there is an extraordinary amount of longing latent in the human fist. I feel it, fortunately, for the most part in retrospect, when I have got home, and it is no longer possible to translate it into action. Sitting in my arm-chair, I have struck more villains in the face, have slapped their cheeks contemptuously and caught them the true, the astronomical blow between the eyes—well, if I told you of all the great hulking brutes I have treated in this way, it would sound like boasting. But, when the great hulking brute is actually standing before me—I don't know why it is, but somehow or other—perhaps you would call it

A Good Hiding

discretion—anyhow, the plain fact is that I do not lay a finger on him. Can it really be true that discretion is the better part of valour? If so, I am wasting my time in civil life. I ought to be Commander-in-Chief of an army.

Let me be just to myself, however. If I suddenly find myself a spectator of some barbarous or brutal incident, I am sometimes surprised into uttering a ferocious yell. When I do utter it no one in the street is more startled than myself. It is a loud, ear-splitting, blood-curdling yell, which expresses all the varying passions of a Grand Guignol play in one note of music. People turn round and stare when they hear it. Others besides myself go pale at the sound. Policemen increase their pace and walk towards me. Motorists crane their necks to see whether they have run over a man or a wild beast. Windows are flung open and heads thrust out. A deadly silence of expectation falls on the neighbourhood, as people listen for a repetition of the sound. Luckily, very few of them know where it came from, or even what caused it. The cat that was being chased by the dog has now escaped through the area railings, and the dog, whose beastly behaviour had made me so excited, is looking round like everybody else to see what the noise is about. As for me, I am doing my best to look as if I had nothing to do with it. I resume the quiet, innocent expression of a man whose voice would not be likely to be louder than a chicken's cheep. Even those who

The Peal of Bells

were within a few feet of me when I yelled are deceived. They stare at me and decide that it must have been somebody else. The policeman alone is not deceived. He stares at me in such a way that I feel he can see my backbone through my chest, and my knees turn to water. He has a perfectly horrid stare. I should like to nod to him and say: "It's all right. It was only a dog chasing a cat"; but I pass on as unconcernedly as possible and say nothing. He is certainly staring abominably. He is obviously wondering whether I yell like that because it is my notion of being funny and he should arrest me for creating a disturbance, or whether I am, perhaps, a lunatic and he should arrest me for that. Good Lord, he is walking after me. I must hurry. This is the last time, I tell myself bitterly, that I shall ever interfere between a cat and a dog. After all, the cat always gets away. Thank Heaven, there's a bus. As I climb the stair, I would, if I dared, turn round and wave good-bye to the policeman, who is now standing still and looking after me. But I do not feel safe until I am in the next suburb. Such are the alarming consequences of a too impulsive chivalry. Nor, I regret to say, is this an isolated incident. It has occurred in Hampstead (several times) and in Highgate, in Battersea and in Kensington. It may be that I was a cat in some previous existence. It is the most reasonable explanation of the extreme horror I feel every time I see a dog chasing a cat across a street.

A Good Hiding

On one or two occasions, I must admit, however, I have yelled on behalf of some human fellow-creature. One day, I was passing down a side street near the Thames, when a great hulking brute—oh, yes, he was all that—rushed at a smaller man and began to pound his head unmercifully. Before I had time to think, I found myself yelling at the top of my voice—yelling so terribly that the great hulking brute dropped his victim like a hot potato—which, by the way, is very seldom dropped—at least, not at the best tables—and glared round to see who had addressed him. When he saw that it was I, his eyes began to roll and he gnashed his teeth in a horrible fashion. "Who the hell are *you*?" he said, jutting out his jaw savagely. "Some day you'll get what you're asking for." Now, some of you may know what answer I ought to have made to him; but I confess I was absolutely tongue-tied. I might, of course, have answered: "Oh, shall I?" in a taunting tone, and bluffed him into thinking that I was a great hulking brute myself. But suppose the bluff failed and he was merely infuriated. In that case, I should probably have got what I was asking for there and then. As for his question, "Who the hell are *you*?" I might have answered him, "Oh, I am Y. Y.!" but even that might have annoyed him. Looking back on the affair, I feel I did the wise thing in going on smoking and saying nothing and slipping off down the street as quietly as possible. Meanwhile, the little man had run for his life and

The Peal of Bells

had got away safely. The row, I think, was connected with some strike or other, and I fancy the wretch that my yell saved was a blackleg. It would be tedious to recount the other occasions on which I have been surprised into shrieking, roaring, yelling, bellowing—I don't think there is any verb in English that describes it accurately—by the spectacle of man's inhumanity to man. There was that terrifying night near King's Cross, for instance, when in the dark distance a young man began to thump the girl with whom he was walking. At the sound of the yell, he stopped beating her at once, but, instead of walking away quietly, as I hoped, he waited for me on the pavement. "Good God!" I thought to myself, "this is the end. This is awful." And I never wished more ardently that I had been taught boxing instead of trigonometry. To my relief, as I approached, he called out in a nervous voice: "It's all right, guv'nor." I said to him, in an equally nervous voice: "You know you shouldn't strike a woman." He repeated in an easier and even good-natured tone: "It's all right, guv'nor." Infected by his reviving courage and good nature, I urged: "You won't strike her again, will you?" He again made the same reply: "It's all right, guv'nor," and he and the girl walked off in silence down the dark and melancholy street. . . . Now, ought I to have given him a good hiding? To put it more accurately, ought I to have attacked him in such a way as would have ensured his giving me a good hiding? Life is

A Good Hiding

full of such dilemmas for those who from an early age have neglected their biceps. There are, I know, men who make up for the smallness of their biceps by the greatness of their spirit, and who, in the magnanimity of their wrath, would fling themselves on a lion, and defeat it, too. There was David who overcame Goliath. Yes, I should like to be—— Yes, but, hang it all, that is even a wilder daydream than the daydream of being Carpentier.

Sometimes my ambition dwindles, and, instead of wishing that I could give somebody a good hiding, I should be content merely to be able to persuade a great hulking brute to go away. If you have ever sat in a house waiting for a great hulking brute, probably maddened with drink, who is expected to call, you will realize how one longs at such a time for the gift of quiet persuasion. One afternoon, on paying a visit to a lady and her daughter, I found myself greeted enthusiastically with a cry of "Oh, you can help us to keep guard"; and they both said how good it was to have a man in the house. I did not like the sound of this, and I felt still more alarmed when I was told that Mrs. Smith, the washerwoman, was sitting downstairs in the kitchen with a black eye, that her husband, a great ruffian of a navvy, had been drinking for a week, that he had threatened to break every bone in her body, that she had come here for refuge, and that she was expecting him to come after her. "We mustn't let him in at any cost," said the lady. "If he comes, *you* had better open the door. A bully is always more afraid of another man." On this point I did not agree with her, but I could not tell her so without appearing to wish to put a woman into the post of danger. I did suggest, indeed: "Don't you think it would be better not to open the door at all? Then he would think there was nobody in and go away." But the lady said that it was always best to face a bully and let him see that you were not afraid of him. "Besides," she said, "you can tell him exactly what you think of a man who beats his wife. I shouldn't spare him," she added; "Smith is a gentleman who needs to be told the truth." I sat down, feeling very pessimistic, and at intervals murmured the Lord's Prayer quietly to myself while the lady and her daughter went on talking with more and more animation. They became quite gay as they looked forward to the lesson that Smith was going to be taught; I heard their conversation only in scraps, I am afraid, for my ears were bestowing all their attention on the front gate that I expected to bang at any moment and to let in Smith. I was also thinking hard, and I was wondering whether any of the weapons that I saw on the wall and on the mantelpiece would be of any use to me. There was the great black club of a Congo chief on the mantelpiece, for instance. I might hit Smith a bump on the head with that, and, while he was lying unconscious, we could send for the police. But suppose Smith disarmed me before I could hit him, and

A Good Hiding

brought the club down on my head with the full force of a navvy hammering a pile into the ground. In that case I should probably be killed. My thoughts turned in preference to an old naval sword that was hanging on the wall. But how the dickens does one use a sword? It is all very well to say "Cut off his head with it" or "Stick him in the stomach with it," but I have a notion that all this needs practice. The sword attracted me, however, for, if I knew how to use it, I could kill Smith; and I wanted to kill Smith. At least, I longed for Smith to be dead. God help me! is that the front gate opening? It is. There are clumping footsteps on the path. "At last," says the lady, with a deep breath of satisfaction. "No," she corrects herself in a disappointed tone, as she looks out of the window, "it's only the grocer's boy." I should like to kill the grocer's boy for giving me such a fright. I hope the others don't hear my heart thumping. I wonder how long I shall be able to stand this. The lady shows me a Greek dagger and makes jokes about it. She takes down a Spanish clasp-knife, and, making a gesture with it, says: "And smote him thus!" And she and her daughter are both greatly amused. Truly, this is the most miserable afternoon I have ever spent in the company of women . . . And, in the end, Smith never came . . .

Looking back on it, I am glad I did not kill him; but I should certainly like to have given him a good hiding. It is, perhaps, just as well that I have no biceps. If I had, I should be scrapping with so many people that I should probably have a permanent black eye. Still, even without a biceps, I ought to have done something to that man who was bullying his dog on Monday night. He did not kick it or anything like that, but the way in which he spoke to it and tugged it by the chain was bullying and brutal. He stopped tugging when he saw he was being looked at. But he was, undoubtedly, a case for a good hiding. I think I should be a happier and a better man if I gave somebody of this kind a good hiding—say, about once a week.

IX. *Horses*

IT is a fact beyond dispute that we read many things in the correspondence columns of newspapers that we should never dream of reading if they appeared in the form of an article. The man who writes an article has an authoritative air, rather like a policeman's, and the official pomp, while it impresses us, does not make for intimacy. He is a public character rather than a human being. He does not let slip his secrets; he imparts only carefully selected information. The man who writes a letter to the paper, on the other hand, has no official standing. He does not speak down to us from a platform, but is more comparable to an interrupter or heckler in the body of the hall at a public meeting. Nine times out of ten the interrupter is a bore, but we always give him the benefit of the doubt and turn round with eager curiosity to hear what he has to say. He is, at least, an odd fish, and is obviously inspired by excitement or egotism or, best of all, stung into utterance by a bee in his bonnet. He speaks for himself alone. He is an embodied whim, and we listen to his questions and opinions for sport rather than for instruction. During a world-crisis, he will write to the papers complaining of the mispronunciation of bus-conductors or to say that he

The Peal of Bells

had seen a bat flying up and down the main street of his village on Christmas Eve. He excites himself over such questions as whether eggs should be sold by weight or by the dozen, and will one day be denouncing the Bolsheviks and the next be boasting of the size of his vegetable-marrow. Nothing human is alien to him, from the deplorable increase in the use of lip-stick to the custom of hanging out coco-nuts for tits in the back garden. The correspondence column, indeed, instead of being the pulpit of the writer, is the confessional of the reader. And, because we cannot help believing that every human being has it in him to write at least one good letter to a paper, we go on hopefully dipping into the letters day after day in spite of a thousand past disappointments.

Those who read the "Points from Letters" in the *Times* were rewarded recently by a peculiarly fascinating letter on "Long-Distance Rides." It was bald enough in manner, and was quite free from any amusing element of the ridiculous, but it was a sincere confession of pleasure that must have changed the face of England for a number of people as they read it. It was written by a gentleman who lives in Lincolnshire and who set out on horseback one day last spring on a journey to the West of England. His very first sentence makes one feel a hundred years young:

Last April I rode my chestnut mare "Jean" from Spald-

Horses

ing to Gloucester, *via* Shrewsbury. Starting at 9 o'clock on the Sunday morning, I arrived in Gloucester at 4.30 p. m. the following Wednesday. Two days later I left Gloucester at 10 o'clock, journeying *via* Leicester, and eventually returning to Spalding, which I reached rather late (about 10 o'clock) on the evening of Monday, the 9th. As my weight is rather heavy (about 15 st.) I had very little gear, which I carried in a haversack, and, like Captain Browne, I avoided the main roads as much as possible.

Is it not as though a lost England had burst into leaf again? Here, at least, is one man of fifteen stone who in the most practical manner possible denies the existence of the twentieth century. He emerges, a peculiar figure, in these fuliginous days, and in an instant we pass through the smoke with him and his chestnut mare "Jean" into the blessed air of a Sunday morning in April, bright above an enchanted land, in which long roads stretch out in the sun in a silence that is seldom broken but by the sweet music of horseshoes and the rumble of unhurrying wheels. I do not suppose that England ever actually enjoyed that golden peace of which we conjure up a vision when we imagine the age of machinery undone and the roads given back to horses. But no one who was born before the invention of the motor-car can help looking back covetously to a time in which, on many a long day, the world seemed almost to stand still as it received the benediction of the sun. True, at the time, we admired the horse for his swiftness; but now, when it is too late, we realize that his great merit was his slowness and that his easy ambling trot as he took us to church or market set the pace for time. In those days we used to sing on Sunday mornings:

> I joyed when to the house of God
> Go up they said to me.

If I experienced this joy, it was at times, I fear, less on account of the sermon than because I used to go up to the house of God seated behind a dark brown horse with a star in his forehead, holding the reins and clicking him into a trot with my tongue. If I had money and lived in the country to-day, I am shamefully aware that I should keep not a horse but a motor-car. I cannot resist the times and live deliberately in a world of horses that has ceased to exist. But when I read of someone else doing this, I feel an aching desire to open a door into an old vanished world in which the proudest throne for a small child was the bare back of a horse going down to the pond to drink. How exquisitely novel was the sensation when the horse advanced into the water and drank as though he could drain the pond at a draught! It was a giddy perch as one looked down the long declivity of his neck. There, in the midst of the water, one was for the moment islanded and cut off from the human race. I was never a horseman, but even for the sake of those brief rides from the stable to the pond, my hands grasping the mane and the halter-rope, I count that world ill lost.

Horses

Those were days, indeed, in which I would have gone anywhere with a horse. I was happy walking after him beside the plough, and, if I grew tired, I could lie down under the hedge and be happy merely watching him to the other side of the field and back again, and then again, and then again, and so on till teatime, with no sound to break the quiet but a lark singing in the air or a bee passing, or an occasional sharp distant cry from the ploughboy, a tyrant giving orders to his pet and his slave. Equally delightful it was to go anywhere in a cart, whether to the rivermouth for a load of sand, or into the meadow to bring back a load of hay to the stack-garden, or into the town to fetch bags of fertilizers from the railway station or flour from the miller's. Even to be given a ride in a cart, when one was walking along the road into town, was to add to the happiness of life. "Have a sail?" the farm-labourer who was driving would call out, for in that part of the world to ride was to "sail" and to walk was to "travel." (Thus, if a man were asked "How did you get home last night, John?" his answer would be "Joe Campbell gave me a sail," or "I travelled," according to whether he had driven home or walked.) A small boy in the country enjoys few things better than to be given a sail in an old blue and red cart that goes lumbering along the ruts in the road, slow as a wounded beetle. His spirit is not jarred, though his body may be, as the cart bumps from stone to stone in tracks that wriggle like sound-waves and that are deepened a fraction more by every new cart that passes. The walking horse progresses at so easy a pace that every now and then the cart seems to stand still for a second, and the animal's feet strike the road slowly as the tolling of a bell. But you would not have it go faster. You could sit all day watching the horse's back, its moving shoulders, its hairy feet, the little swellings of its veins, the skin that quivers where it had just been bitten by a horse-fly, the swing of its barbered tail under the irritation, the impatience of its head as the flies gather on its neck, the old worn harness frayed and held together with string, the driver smoking a clay pipe and occasionally pausing in the middle of his questions to cry "Hupp!" and give the rope reins in his hand a gentle shake. There is no advantage in driving in a cart in these circumstances save that one is sitting behind a horse. You could walk as fast and, if you did, you would feel less tired at the end of your journey. But walking is an exercise without pomp or luxury, whereas to drive even in the dirtiest blue and red cart is to be a lord of creation on whose moving chariot the sun shines.

Hence it was, no doubt, pure selfishness that made me as a child such a lover of horses and so confirmed a frequenter of the stable. I could still go into it, I think, and point out the stall in which each horse stood and remember its name. Three generations of cart horses stood side by side in it—Bell, the grey mare, now so aged that her marbled skin was turned

Horses

to a freckled white; Moll, her black daughter, quiet and powerful, with great hairy feet; and Lofty, the son of Moll, a great gawky, overgrown bay, with bones that stuck out like apples, and a backbone so sharp that it was quite painful to be given a ride on him on the way out to the field. Then there was Ned of the hairless feet, of the colour known as dark brown, but really black, with a white star in his forehead, who was a driving-horse on Sundays and for going to the station or to market, but who could do his turn between the shafts of a cart when necessary. He had bolted in his youth, causing an accident that got into the papers, but he was now so submissive that even I could be trusted to drive him. "Drive him on a sweet rein," my uncle would tell me, showing me how to keep the reins at a proper tautness; and nothing pleased me more, when my uncle was not there, than to drive Ned to such purpose that he would break into a gallop along an empty road under the stars. Night, I am sure, is the pleasantest of all times for driving a horse. He is hungry and eager for home, and willing to collaborate in any plan for getting there quickly, and to enter into the excitement of an escapade in the dark.

It was not Ned, but his miserable bay successor—a lazy but nervous pony—who made a public exhibition of me in the town one day, when I had been left alone with him outside a shop. He suddenly began to stand on his hind legs between the shafts

The Peal of Bells

at the bray of a donkey, and I, sitting behind him, saw him towering above me like a cliff, as I seemed to sink back into nowhere. I spoke to him in as reasonable a tone as I could assume, and touched him gently with the whip, but again and again he reared and sent me down, down, like a bucket into a well. What a fool one feels to be so treated in a public place! How afraid one is—at least, how afraid I was—that one may have gone white, and that one may not be looking as calm as a novitiate man ought to look when a handful of belated rescuers gather round the horse's head! Much more did I feel at home with Maggie, the twenty-year-old bay mare, as round as a barrel, who had been used for driving in her prime, but was now reduced to light work in a cart. On sunny evenings she was sometimes saddled for me, and I set out for the perils of the road, warned in advance not to tire her by trotting. I obeyed as well as a boy could. But when we had ambled down the lane, and, after that, down the hill to Craig's farm, which was so steep that she almost sat on her haunches and slid down to the bottom of it, and turned off the main road into the solitude of the Green Lane, it was a temptation to give a little flick of the riding-whip and remind her that she, too, was once young and could jog merrily between the hedges. Perhaps I should have ridden her harder, but I was afraid of that reproachful look when I got home, and the accusation, more in sorrow than in anger: "You've been trotting her. She's sweating."

Horses

Hence, she had never trotted many yards when I called, "Whoa!" to her, and patted her on the neck, as though reproving her for too much friskiness, and we advanced at a walking-pace towards the trees round Quilly farm. To her and to the grey mare, Bell, on whose back I had also many a slow sunset ride past farmhouse and cornfield, in sight of the river and the sea, I owe, perhaps, my love of the walking-pace and my incapacity to feel quite at home in an age of motor-cars. They are both dead these many years—dead as the age in which they walked in cart or in saddle along quiet and dusty roads, with no hoot of motor-horn to bid them make way for their conquerors and supplanters.

One man in England, I think, will sympathize with my regrets for them and for green-bordered roads so silent and so solitary. He weighs fifteen stone and lives in Lincolnshire.

X. *In Defence of Patent Medicines*

HOW few people there are who are fair in their attitude to patent medicines! Almost everybody takes them, but scarcely anybody speaks of them without derision. If a man likes—nay, loves—roast duckling, he will confess his taste to the world as though it were something to boast about. If he enjoys tobacco or red wine, he will talk about them by the hour to anyone for whom he really cares. The conversation will come and go in little warm waves of happy understanding that meet and leap as they cross each other, so much is to be said on these great subjects. But if you speak in praise of a patent medicine in company, you will only invite ridicule. Everybody will pretend to be incredulous, and even the quiet little man in the corner who says nothing and makes a note in his mind to go round to the chemist's in the morning and buy a bottle will pretend to join in the laugh with the rest. This is surely not quite honest. If men were all really sceptics about patent medicines, it would obviously not pay to advertise pills and potions day after day in the newspapers, and chemists would not be so much commoner than booksellers. It is a moderate estimate that fifty people buy patent medicines for one who buys books. Yet a man can praise Mr.

In Defence of Patent Medicines

Conrad in talk without raising a smile, whereas, if he goes about trying to persuade everybody to use Zang, the great cure for pains in the shoulders, he will soon get the reputation of an odd creature. I, for one, having little reputation to lose, intend henceforth to be bold about the matter, and I herewith confess myself a devoted adherent of patent medicines. The taste, I think, is inherited. I grew up in an environment of shelves of books and shelves of medicine bottles, and I found myself at an early age stretching up a tiny hand for the treasures of both. I do not know which I learned to love first—Hans Andersen's "Ugly Duckling" or sugar-coated pills. I remember that I had to stand on a chair to reach either of them, for Hans Andersen was, as luck had it, on a top shelf, which may have made him the more desirable. The pills, however, were not only on a top shelf, but in a cupboard with a glass door, and that, too, was attractive. There they stood, pretty, shining and tempting—charming as eggs that had been laid under the rafters of Noah's Ark, and delicious as sweetmeats—huddled together in a little flat circular box that had itself the air of a toy. I fancy the eye of a child is attracted by almost anything that is small and round. How we loved pellets of shot, making little crooked courses for them in the school-desk and becoming so absorbed in the journeys on which we sent them racing that the arithmetic master could recall our attention only with a shout that made us jump! It was the same passion for

The Peal of Bells

the small and the round that made many of us in childhood, when a whole cod was on the dinner-table, ask humbly and hopefully for one or both of the fish's eyes. There may be men who have never known what a pleasure it is to sit looking at the eye of a dead fish on the edge of the plate through a course at dinner. I have heard a nurse reproving small children for so disgusting a taste, and I was shocked as though she were giving them a first lesson in atheism. For the love of the round is the love of perfection; and the earth and the stars, which are shaped like a fish's eye, incite us to it. I cannot say that it was religious enthusiasm that primarily led me to half-carry and half-push the chair over to the medicine-cupboard and to stand up on it and peer into the secrets of the pill-box. But I am sure, if the pills had been shaped less like the worlds that were created during the first week—if they had been flat or square or conical—I should not have unlidded the boxes that contained them so eagerly or so often.

Even then I did not all at once go so far as to "take" the pills. I had always looked on this as a dangerous procedure which women and children had better leave alone. My aunt used to gaze on my uncle with awe whenever he took a pill, swallowing it with the merest sip of water, and she often told me that she did not know how he did it, giving me the impression that it was a scarcely less heroic exploit than that of my theological uncle when he fought the tinker. We did not dare to speak while

In Defence of Patent Medicines

the pill was being swallowed. We watched till it was safely down, almost rigid with apprehension, as those spectators must have felt who saw Blondin crossing Niagara on a tight-rope. To this day I cannot swallow a pill without a moment of excited doubt whether it is in my throat or my windpipe. Naturally, then, I began experimenting with pills only in the timidest fashion. Those that were blackish I did not even taste, but one day I must have put one of the white globes into my mouth and found that in its first flavour it resembled a sugar almond. But, after it had been in the mouth for a minute or so, what a sudden change! I have grown fond of bitter medicine since those days, but even now I can scarcely forbear making a face when I remember my disgust on first discovering what a pill tasted like when the sugar had been sucked through. I do not know what may be the flavours of gall and wormwood, but I fancy they must be something like the inside of that first pill. Practice makes perfect, however, and I became so cunning, in my later raids on my uncle's medicine shelves, that I was in time able to suck all, or nearly all, the sugar off his pills without more than a faint hint on the tongue of the bitterness concealed within. As I always threw the rest of the pill out of the window, you might think that my uncle would before long have noticed the depletion of his boxes and have made perilous inquiries. Like all true devotees of patent medicines, however, he bought a great many more pills and

The Peal of Bells

bottles than one man could consume. You will have observed that, if a man is fond of books, he is constantly buying books that at the time he intends to read but in fact never does read. In the same way the lover of medicines is constantly being lured into the purchase of cure-alls, of which, after the first dose, he forgets the very existence on his shelves. I have seen in my uncle's study a volume still uncut after a dozen years, and he accumulated medicines with the same generous carelessness and pleasure in the mere purchase. After all, the ordinary man who is in fairly good health changes his opinion from day to day as to the disease with which he is most desperately threatened. The bottle that he buys to-day for heart-disease will be of no use to-morrow when he decides that something is wrong with his liver. I myself remember buying a bottle of Swamp-root, but, long before there was time to get through it, I had completely forgotten the illness that I had supposed myself to be suffering from and was off on the track of some other disease, much rarer and more dangerous. I can also remember going into a chemist's for a bottle of Warner's Safe Cure, but, two days after I had taken my treasure home, my mood had changed, and another three-quarters-full bottle was added to my collection.

There may be men with so little of the idealist in their natures that they will condemn such an accumulation of unfinished bottles as an imbecile extravagance. I think they are in error. I sometimes

In Defence of Patent Medicines

wonder whether the bottles of medicine that I finished or the bottles that I left unfinished did me the greater good. The virtue of a medicine probably lies to a considerable extent in the will to get well with which one purchases it. Besides, very often, the only way to counteract the effect of the advertisement is to go out and buy the remedy that is advertised. There are only two of the advertised remedies, I fancy, that I have ardently longed for and that yet I had never the courage to obtain for myself. One was a cure for blushing. Had it been called Nonblusho and sold in packets at chemists' shops I think I should have tried a shillingsworth of it. But, so far as I can remember, one had to write for it, and I could not sit down and write on so delicate a subject to a stranger. I could not face the possibility that the letter might be opened by a lady clerk who would laugh jeeringly. I might, of course, have begun my letter: "Dear Sir, I have a cousin who blushes a great deal," and asked for the remedy as if for another. But I was all simplicity and slow to think of such subtle devices. The other remedy I never dared to send for was a machine for curing ugly or misshapen noses. I do not know how widespread is the misery of noses, but, when I was a child, I would have taken almost anybody's nose in exchange for my own. I once fought a boy over an insult to my nose, and it was none the better as a result of his overwhelming victory. I used to be told that I had had a bad fall on it in infancy, and even the friendliest of my friends treated it as a matter for which I needed to be consoled rather than to be praised. Hence, when I reached the age at which one reads the advertisements in papers, I used to be filled with longing when I came to the advertisement about ugly or misshapen noses. But here again the dread of ridicule prevented me from writing; and now I shall go to my grave without that lean and delicate bridge to my nose that, if I had been given three wishes by a fairy, would once have been one of my choices.

I suppose the nose-machine can in strictness hardly be called a patent medicine; but it appeals to the same love of the ideal. The electric brush for which I paid I forgot how much as a cure for baldness is in the same category; and, like a patent medicine, it lies on my shelves honoured but unused. The world is so full of a number of things that most of us simply have not the time to make use of half the remedies we bring into the house. Do not despise them, however. They represent for us, even though the dust gathers on them, the ideal of getting well and the ideal of looking well, and it is an inspiration to come on them suddenly in moments of depression. I confess that, having a vein of Scottish blood in me, I have scruples that these things should go unused, and I have often tried to persuade others to finish the bottles that I had failed to get through myself. I even made earnest supplications to a friend to try the electric brush that I had got for baldness as a cure for his rheumatism. After all, few of these things can hurt anybody. I remember my uncle had a great black instrument shaped rather like a bassoon which, instead of blowing into, as you would into a musical instrument, he inhaled from in deep breaths. It was, I believe, a cure for asthma, and he had not asthma, but he had smoker's throat, and that served. When at length he grew tired of it and it was laid aside for good in the medicine cupboard, I used privately in his absence to take it out of its long box and draw in deep breaths from it myself. It had a pleasant, sweet, cool taste, somewhat like a cachou; and it made an agreeable change from the monotony of too many sugar-coated pills.

You will understand, then, why I write enthusiastically in defence of patent remedies. I have enjoyed so many of them, and I do not remember any of them ever doing me any harm. I avoid only medicated wines, for I do not like to mix my pleasures. I have a friend who is a teetotaller and who speaks highly of medicated port. Not being a teetotaller, however, I like medicine to look and taste a little less like the sort of thing one drinks for amusement in a public-house.

XI. *Looking for an Ancestor*

IT is one of the minor tragedies of life that there are not enough ancestors to go round. There is a great demand for ancestors, but the supply is so limited that it is quite common to meet people who could not give you the name, address and occupation even of their father's grandfather.

Occasionally, you will meet a self-made man who pretends that he is indifferent to this sort of thing, and that he would much rather be an ancestor than have one. Do not believe him. Every man is the happier, if even the heel-taps of Norman blood are mingled with his own; and if he can trace his line back to some gentleman who led his tenants to the wars five hundred years ago, be sure he will let his friends know about it. I do not say this as one who possesses a genealogical tree from which golden fruits can be had for the plucking. I do not know the name of my father's grandfather, and I do not know whether anybody else knows it. I will not pretend, however, that I would not give five shillings to know it. I remember, when I was a boy, some people came over the sea, looking for an ancestor of our name, and offering us an estate in America if we could prove that we were next-of-kin to a man called Y., who had settled there in the eighteenth

Looking for an Ancestor

century. How eagerly we set about looking for our lost progenitor, up hill and down dale, by lake and lilied stream, not disdaining the humblest cot in our search! We sought him with laughter; we sought him with longing—at least, with longing for his piece of land. But at the end of it all there was no ancestor to be found. We could not discover, indeed, so much as a skeleton in the cupboard. For some time afterwards I had great hopes of a skeleton. I tried to think of some agreeable explanation of my paucity of ancestors, and the most agreeable explanation that occurred to me was that my great-great-grandfather had been hanged for treason and that his immediate descendants, having turned loyalist, had said as little as possible about him, and had allowed all traces of him to disappear. I was a fanatical loyalist myself at the time, but none the less I fervently hoped that my great-great-grandfather had been hanged as a rebel. Such occurrences, to the mind of a boy, add a touch of romantic distinction to the family history. Perhaps, too, I wished to have an ancestral portrait in violent contrast to that of another great-great-grandfather who, when the rebels came to his house by night, and threatened to burn it unless he joined them, went to an upper window and told them to do what they would, for he was a faithful subject of King George. I felt reasonably proud of the old gentleman, as I pictured him at the window aweing the pike-armed horde by the sheer virtue of his attitude into going away and leaving him alone; but I should have been glad of a wilder strain in my blood to dilute with the virtue of so good a citizen. Perhaps it was the same longing for an element of wildness that made me impatient of any explanation that my ancestors had been Scotsmen or Englishmen. I was firmly convinced that Scotsmen and Englishmen were the best and wisest people on earth, and I knew that I had some of their blood in my veins; but they did not seem to me to be sufficiently extraordinary or like the characters in a fairy-tale to make me wish to be descended from them. The love of strangeness is deeply rooted in most of us, and, as I sought the clue to the origins of our family, I was never satisfied with any explanation that brought us from anywhere nearer than France or Spain. I do not know who told me the story, and I fancy it was told in order to pull my leg, but I believed for a long time that we were the offshoots of a Spaniard who had been cast ashore when one of the ships of the Armada had been wrecked near Dunluce Castle. I never asked whether he was a Don or only a common sailor, and I did not care. To have been a Spaniard, and to have been shipwrecked—to have been shipwrecked where now stand those haunted ruins on a steep and sea-beaten tooth of rock—seemed to me far beyond any nominal nobility. Indeed, in my search of an ancestor, I do not think I ever was tempted down a by-way in the hope of coming on a title. I took it for granted that among my multi-

Looking for an Ancestor

tude of relations there were neither dukes nor kings, and I was not an aristocrat even in my dreams. True, at the age of seven, another boy and I conferred titles on ourselves, and, when we exchanged Christmas cards, I wrote on mine: "To Sir D. D. from Lord Y. Y.," and he wrote on his: "To Lord Y. Y. from Sir D. D." But, by the time I was ten, I had cast off all titles as childish things, and had ceased to ask the right to boast of anything grander in the social scale than that I was related to farmers.

I was reminded of the genealogical researches of my boyhood recently, when the post brought me a letter from someone who makes a practice of copying legal documents, informing me that there are more than 10,000,000 documents in the Record Office relating to early Chancery proceedings, and that "among them is the following affecting the Y. family," of which he would make me a full copy for a small sum of money:

Petitioner.	Defendant.	Subject of Proceedings.	Approximate Date.
Thomas Y, esquire	William Wadon	Manor of Chesham, Co. Bucks.	1468

A note had been scribbled at the side, explaining that "the title esquire was very rare in those days," and, though Thomas Y. spelt his surname with an "e" at the end, that does not prove that he is not

The Peal of Bells

the ancestor I had been looking for, because in the year 1468 nobody knew much about spelling. I do not say that I am absolutely convinced that Thomas Y. and I are blood relations, but the fact that he was an esquire (which was a very rare title in those days), and the fact that he had apparently some claim to the Manor of Chesham, are to me strong arguments in favour of the supposition. For all that, I do not think I shall send for a copy of the Chancery proceedings. Our claim to the Manor of Chesham (if, as I presume, there once was a claim) has almost certainly lapsed after four and a half centuries. Hence, I shall content myself, when the spring comes, with spending my Saturday afternoons in the neighbourhood, and entertaining myself with the fancy that I am strolling round the family estate. In moments of bitterness I may curse Thomas because he muddled his and, incidentally, my rights away and bequeathed to his distant descendant nothing but the right to work for a living. But, if the sun is shining, I shall probably be a model of charity and, as I look through the gates up the drive, I shall make a fine act of renunciation and apostrophize the present occupants, bidding them rest in peace, since, charming as I think it, Buckinghamshire is not my favourite county. It may be, of course, that Thomas had no claim to the manor at all, and that he was merely a base curmudgeon suing for a small debt. I shall never inquire. I shall not disturb the dust of so dead a man. I am content to know that

Looking for an Ancestor

someone of my name was living hundreds of years ago, and apparently doing very well for himself. This, you may think, is but a poor farthing of vanity. But, in the matter of ancestors as in other things, beggars cannot be choosers. And, after all, who has not experienced a pleasant titillation of the fancy on coming on his own name unexpectedly on an old tombstone, or in some ancient historical record? At the sight, the imagination leaps into another century, and not only your name, but your very self, seems for the moment to become the inhabitant of a vanished age. So real are names to us. Would not all the Joneses be immensely proud if some Hebrew scholar discovered that Jones was the surname of one of the sons-in-law of Noah?

Hence I do not blame myself unduly for having enjoyed finding Thomas after such a wilderness of years, merely because we share the same surname. Nor do I accuse myself of unnatural pride because, when a day or two later a newspaper arrived with a report of the dedication of an illuminated clock in a church tower in a small country town to a real grandfather, I read the speeches on the occasion, not only with pleasure, but with excitement. Similar speeches are made all over the world every year about other people's relations, and you may be sure that the relations always enjoy them as though such speeches had never been made before. I, for one, could not but feel delighted on being told that on the memorial to a man to whom I was related were the words: "Defender of the people's rights and liberties"; and, when the orator continued: "Their ancestor, fleeing from intolerance and persecution in France, carried with him a love of liberty and hatred of tyranny, which has manifested itself in the life and work of his descendants," it was as though I had suddenly become aware of a forgotten inheritance. Remote churchyards, green after rain, come at such a moment before the imagination, with railed-in tombs that seem to be the repositories of generations of good deeds, and we find ourselves admiring even the sternness that frowns on our degenerate lives from the grave. For one of the odd things about ancestors, even if they are no older than grandfathers, is that we can scarcely help feeling that, compared to them, we are degenerate. This, no doubt, is only a passing mood, and there are other moods in which we criticize a too rigid and reprehending virtue. But whether it is that their blood survives in us and flows in self-approval, or whether it is that we honestly admire virtue, even in its intimidating forms, it is unnatural not to take pride in the dead and reproach ourselves for having been a little—nay, more than a little—faithless to the iron example of their lives. Strange, how comparatively meaningless their lives seem in some respects to us to-day. Here, clipped from the newspaper, for instance, is the record of one great-grandfather: "In the year 1818, when the Burgher and Anti-Burgher Synods were united to form the

Looking for an Ancestor

United Secession Church, he was appointed its first Moderator." God knows I do not even know what the words mean. Burgher and Anti-Burgher are more unreal to me than Montague and Capulet and are as the names of two rival factions in a forgotten riot. Even so, and though I dislike sects and cannot quite approve of my relative's troubling his head about them, I find myself admiring his worth, and I all but share the pleasure he must have felt in being appointed first Moderator of the United Secession Church. Heavens, what a name for a church! I wonder what Thomas Y. would have thought of it. Truly, ancestors are of all sorts. I speak as one who has few, but who does his best to be proud of them all.

XII. *Heat*

THERE was a time when, for a year or so, I sat in a class-room and studied heat, light, sound and electricity. I never succeeded, unfortunately, in learning much about the nature of any of them, for a number of high-spirited young men with a pronounced anti-scientific bias—with a bias, indeed, against learning of any kind whatsoever—sat in the back benches and devoted their energies on the opening day to the manufacture of paper darts which they hurled at the head of the professor who was lecturing. He was an aged man with jerky movements and a jerky voice and a white beard that streamed like a flag in the wind. Strange that youth should find pleasure in persecuting age in this fashion, but it may be that the young men meant to be merciless, not to the old man, but to the professor. "Gentlemen, gentlemen," he would appeal, and then, with a wave of his tremulous hand, cry, "Put them out, Jackson," to the porter who remained at his side to help him with his apparatus. This, it must be admitted, was not an atmosphere conducive to sober inquiry into the nature of things. Whether it is for this reason or for some other, I am still so ignorant on these matters that I should have to look up in a book before I could explain

Heat

why it is hotter in summer than in winter or—a still more difficult problem—why it is sometimes colder in summer than in winter. Men of science, I understand, say that these things are governed by law, but those of us who know no science can see no trace of order in a scheme of things that cuts us to the bone with the cold wind one July and melts us like melted butter the next. The days are undoubtedly longer in summer than in winter, but, apart from this, there is no certainty in the seasons. Who could have foretold a month ago that by this time we should be sweltering under a cloudless sky as we used to swelter in the summers of our childhood? Life is full of surprises, but there is nothing more permanently surprising than the English summer. It surprises us when it is cold; it surprises us when it is hot; it surprises us even when it is lukewarm. Whether it bursts upon us in May or in June or in July, it comes on us as unexpectedly as if a millionaire whom we had never met suddenly began to shower his gold on us. It is the genius of the summer to restore us to the Golden Age when men lay lazily under the trees, and crimson-cheeked fruits fell all around them with a plump, so that they had not even to take the trouble to rise out of their lethargy in order to pick them. The anthropologists of our time have attempted to destroy this happy picture of the life of primitive man, and to put in his place a stunted, semi-articulate creature little more enviable in shape or in diet than a baboon. I prefer

The Peal of Bells

the evidence of the poets on this point, and I shall continue to think of primitive man as a beautiful and indolent creature in a tennis-shirt and white trousers stretched under a fruit tree by the bank of a purling stream with little crystal waves breaking among the grasses at the bend of the water.

Primitive man, indeed, as the old poets saw, was man before the curse of work fell upon him. He was man as we see him to-day at Henley, young, rich, idle, and happy. How cool it makes one even to think of him in that scene of tree-shadows and running water! The coloured balloons that float above the punts at Henley—what are they but memories of the lovelier fruits of his lost Paradise? It is a curious fact that one can think of the Golden Age only as an age populated by rich young men and rich young women. They may indulge in the energies of sport but not of work. The vulgar servitude of earning one's bread in the sweat of one's brow is the mark of our fallen nature. If, every summer, men and women congregate at Henley, at Goodwood, at Cowes, it is but their make-believe that they are back in the ancient world of green and white and blue, that they have no more duties than children or than angels, and that winds and waters and grassy downs exist but to give them a place of pleasure. Even though I have never been rich and am never likely to be rich so long as the authorities continue to prohibit sweepstakes, I confess that I, too, feel extraordinarily happy in these scenes in which

Heat

the idle rich take their pleasure. How beautiful is that phrase, "the idle rich"! It has been used for the most part as a term of abuse, but I will never use it so. Who am I to abuse the idle rich, when to be idle and rich is an amusement in which I would so willingly take part myself? How charming a man was William Morris to invent a Socialist Utopia in which everybody was idle and rich, or at least in which labour was but a delightful way of making use of leisure, and all the citizens of the nation might have lolled in cushioned punts at Henley!

It is a strange fact, however, that heat is associated in the popular imagination not only with Utopia but with its opposite. Heaven and Hell are, in the thoughts of most people, both hot places. I do not know why this should be except that they both begin with an H. The belief in the heat of Hell, however, is by no means universal. The Hell of the ancient Irish was a cold place where the ice did not melt. They did not squander on the Devil so sacred an element as fire. Even so logical a race as the Irish have, since that time, yielded to the general view of Christendom, as was seen when a Southern Unionist—quoting, I believe, an earlier authority—said that they would fight Home Rule till Hell froze and then they would go on fighting till the ice broke. To him, ice was a contradiction of Hell instead of its conclusive sign. On the other hand, though the picture of Hell has wavered between heat and cold, I do not think there have ever been

The Peal of Bells

two opinions about Heaven. In Heaven it is always summer. Every Utopia, every lotus-land, of which men dream is a place of summer fruits and sunny skies. This, it seems to me, is natural. Summer is the time of the fullness of life in fruit and flower. It is probable that we, too, bloom under the auspicious sun. I met a poet during the week who declared that a heat-wave always filled him with energy and that he could work harder at such a time than during any other part of the year. If others of us feel limp instead of buoyant just now, it is, I fancy, because we are engaged in some less heavenly pursuit than writing poetry. Summer fits us for the work we love—writing poetry, playing tennis and such things—and makes the work we hate doubly hateful. The true test of whether we love our work or not is whether we can do it even better in summer than in winter. Winter is an excellent season for routine-work. Even the dull, daily round seems a release from the brutality of the cold outside. Men often tell you that they feel brisk in winter. This only means that in a cold and dismal world they would rather be working than doing anything else. They seek forgetfulness of their miserable surroundings, and there are only two sure means of forgetfulness known to man—work and drink—and, of the two, work is the more economical. I should not like to speak ill of work. I agree with the preachers that it is an excellent discipline for those who need discipline. But, how-

Heat

ever hard I try and however I picture to myself the activities of Paradise, I cannot imagine anyone's being set to clerking or navvying there. Modern spiritualists do, it is true, hint occasionally at a future life in which the workers of this world go on being the workers of the next, but Heaven, in the imaginations of most of us, is a complete change, and in nothing more than in the fact that the angels do no hack-work. It is not, I think, that men wish to be absolutely indolent, but that they wish to be busy as a prince or a poet is busy or as a moderately rich man is busy during a summer holiday.

It is only when the warm summer weather comes that we remember that the object of all civilization should be to make life more and more of a holiday—in other words, to make the activities of all men and women, as far as is possible, enjoyments. If science and invention cannot in a measure take the burden of hack-work off the shoulders of men and women and release them for activities that will make them happy, the men of science and the inventors will have been a doubtful boon. I should not advocate a life of exclusive pleasure—of wine, women and song, in the old phrase—for that, apparently, is the way to melancholy. But, as the perspiration drops from my brow, I do feel that a little more poetry, a little more seaside, and a little more Ascot, should be the portion of the common life of man. Alas! poor mortals, we are

The Peal of Bells

so incapacitated by the long cold of winter that most of us are unable to enjoy the summer sea when we have the chance. We build Brightons and Bournemouths and Margates in order to defend ourselves against the perfect beauty of blue seas. We take shops and chimneys with us down to the edge of the ocean in order that our surroundings may not be too unlike the surroundings of our winter servitude. All the aids to forgetfulness are there—picture-palaces, music-halls, billiard-rooms and bar-rooms—as though in presence of sea and sun there were any need of forgetfulness. We have become such ding-dong slaves that we can no longer enjoy the heat of midsummer, but must continue the habits of the gloomy town even in our holidays. And, in this matter, do not rush to the conclusion that I claim any superiority over the rest of my kind. Do you think that I shall be able to keep out of the casino next month? Do you think that I shall be able to resist the lure of the picture-palace by the sea in August? Have I chosen a rustic solitude or an hotel with "good cuisine" as a refuge from the year's drudgery? Ah! do not inquire too closely. The cuisine, I trust, will be up to expectations. Good cooking, a blue sea, and a blazing sun—are they not all ingredients of the happiness of a weaker brother?

XIII. *Experiences of a Voter*

IT is a remarkable fact—remarkable, at least, to me—that I have never in my life voted at a Parliamentary election. Men have died, and worms have eaten them, in order that I might have a vote. But I might as well be living under Peter the Great for all the use I have ever made of the vote that I possess. My blood has boiled on occasion at the denial of votes to other people, mainly women. Yet no woman was ever in practice more disfranchised than I. If I were interviewed to-morrow by a stranger from Mars on the manners and customs of the modern world, I should have to confess that I was ignorant of the most characteristic of them, for I have never cast a vote and I have never ridden a bicycle. But stay, I once voted in an election for a Board of Guardians. I doubt if any good came of it. I fancy that the other party, whatever it stood for, won. The only other election in which I played even a subsidiary part was a borough council election. I was coming out of a railway station with a friend, when a man in a gig leaned down and said: "Have you voted yet? Come and vote for So-and-so." "I never heard of him," said my friend, "but"—looking down at his heavy portmanteau—"if you drive round past my house and leave this bag in, I'll vote for him with pleasure." "Jump up," said the man, and we climbed in with the bag, and within a quarter of an hour my friend had performed his duty as a democratic citizen. After that, I began to doubt the wisdom of allowing politicians to give free rides to voters on election days. At the same time, I am no cynic in regard to the vote and its uses. I have no doubt that life was worth living before votes were ever thought of, but I am sure life is more comfortable for more people since voting became a practice among civilized men. I have never been able to remain indifferent to the way in which other people vote during even a by-election. I persuade myself, like the most excited partisan, that the fate of this million-year-old star depends upon it. I become as irrational as the clergyman whom I heard preaching during the 1922 election and who said: "Believe me, dear friends, God and His holy angels are looking down with interest in the conduct of, and concern for the result of, the General Election." Not that I would quarrel with this clergyman's point-of-view in general, but his phrasing suggested a certain lack of foresight in Heaven that was to me scarcely credible. He did not exaggerate, however, more than other excitable men always exaggerate during an election. In so far as we are politicians, we cannot help believing that the world can be saved by politics, though, in so far as we are religious men, we know that it cannot be saved without religion,

Experiences of a Voter

and, in so far as we are artists, we are sure that it cannot be saved without the arts. Except at the actual time of an election, I suspect that the importance of politics is greatly exaggerated, but even so I am not sure that it would not be better if men thought them still more important than they do. The human group, like the motor-car, progresses as the result of a series of explosions, and without some highly inflammable stuff this would be impossible. It is no argument against the use of petrol if a motor-car takes us to a destination that disappoints our hopes, and it is no argument against our political enthusiasm that no General Election ever yet carried us to Paradise. If we did not waste a great deal of superfluous excitement on politics, we should probably waste it on something worse. Nature is a spendthrift in all her ways. She wastes human enthusiasms as she wastes the seeds of the lettuce and the turnip. But do not be misled into imagining that she wastes them in vain.

Hence I do not regret as misspent those long hours during which I have stood outside the Town Hall awaiting the result of the poll, and hoping against hope that the impossible had happened, and that the good cause—I shan't tell you what it was—had won. Nor do I regret those other long hours during which I have stood outside the "Bird in Hand" and seen the results of the elections through three kingdoms flashed forth to the eyes of rival choruses of bellowers. Good heavens, how the heart

The Peal of Bells

sang when it was announced that an ex-Cabinet Minister on the other side had fallen prone as Dagon! Lyrics have been written out of tinier joys. How the centre of one's being sank earthwards when it was seen that the great man, the good man, the man on whom we had pinned so much of our faith, had just failed to capture his seat! With what hungry impatience we waited for the result of some particular and doubtful election—an election somewhere in Manchester or Glasgow or even in St. Pancras! On such a night, no candidate who was on our side but was a hero. He may have seemed a poor enough candidate in the colder blood of a week before, but he was now no longer a man, but was apotheosized as the Mercury of our cause. There are people who believe in voting for honest men at all costs during an election. When no election is afoot, I can agree with them. But, when once my electoral blood is up, I fear I should vote for the Devil himself if he came forward as a candidate on my side. I should say: "Give him another chance. Perhaps he's not so black as he's painted." And I should not be unduly outraged to find the hoardings of the constituency plastered with posters bearing the inscription: "Vote for the Devil and a purer public life." I do not say this as one who boasts of his wisdom. For all I know, this may be the most short-sighted folly. But I am in temperament one of those who live in a wild hope that, for once in history, instead of the Devil's being able to make use of the party for his

Experiences of a Voter

own purposes, the party will be able to make use of the Devil for the furtherance of the cause. Alas, not even the Devil dared to come forward on my side during this last election in the constituency in which I happen to live, and an honest man on the wrong side was returned unopposed. That, or something like it, has always been my luck as a voter. I have never lived in a constituency in which there was the slightest possibility of getting rid of the sitting member, and I have never been represented in Parliament by a member with whom I agreed on a single point, except his hostility to Local Veto and his belief in subsidizing all good schools, religious or profane, out of the taxes.

This, you might think, would have damped a potential voter's political ardour. But our politics, if we are politicians, is in our blood, and is not to be expelled by untoward circumstances. A word is spoken, and something in us responds. Pugnacities that we had almost forgotten awake into life, and, perhaps, even the vision that seemed to have perished with our youth is for the moment renewed. I confess I was surprised some time ago when, finding myself in Leeds on a Saturday afternoon, I wandered into a political meeting and under the spell of the spoken word saw the golden age-to-come breaking its way back through the infinities of space and re-creating itself in little lovely golden mists before my eyes. I do not suppose I have much of a conscience left, but there must be some fragments, for I was aware of a curious pricking sensation as the golden age drew nearer and nearer without a hand of mine to help it. Not that the golden age actually came to earth, but it hung suspended in mid-air between the burning face of the orator and the burning faces of the old, middle-aged and young men who sat in rows in the gallery listening to him. Strange that one should be able to go out cheerfully to a long dinner with its sequence of many-shaped glasses, when by scorning delights and living laborious days one might help to speed the building of an earth far lovelier than any heaven that has ever been described in words. It was certainly no mere greed of wages that responded in the audience to the passion of the speaker. It was a longing for a life fuller of the charities for all men's children—of happier homes and honester work and more abundant knowledge, and, above all, in an ugly phrase that yet means better than it says, of mutual service. I went back in memory to a time when I believed that such a world could rise up as if by magic in my own lifetime if only everybody read the *Clarion* and agreed with it. I remembered writing, in the innocence of my enthusiasm: "Ideals give men seven-league boots." Alas! since then I have seen those seven-league boots hastening men to destruction, and I no longer think that anyone should put on seven-league boots unless he has a particularly good head. Otherwise he may become giddy and rush off, dancing-mad, towards his goal. At the same time, though the ideal was visible enough to the eyes of these old, middle-aged and young men whom I saw before me, the orator did not incite them to approach it shod with anything but the ordinary black boots that each of them was wearing. I could not acquit myself, indeed, on the score that I no longer believed in seven-league boots, for it was evident that these men were willing to drudge at the beginnings of something that would take far longer to build than St. Peter's and that no man living would see. My only doubt was whether it was not wrong not to ask for a trowel. If children can be saved by politics from rags and poverty and ignorance and disease and filth; if men and women can be saved from the haunting terror of worklessness and penury; if our race can be passed through a political gate into a world in which every man, instead of going round and round in a narrow circle (as both the poor man and the rich man do to-day), shall be a citizen of the whole shining earth and an heir to all the poets and painters and musicians and men of knowledge as well as to the fruits of the field—if all this can be achieved by politics, it seems treason to stand aloof. I am not sure, however, that this really can be achieved by even the most miraculous politics alone. Just as some men injured goodness by believing that the world could be saved by goodness alone, and as others injured beauty by believing that the world could be saved by beauty alone, so, I fancy, politics would lose rather than gain if we allowed ourselves to become convinced that in politics alone we can find the key to the salvation of mankind. Hence, perhaps, it does not matter so much after all that I was not able to vote on Thursday, and it may matter just as little that, though I can still see the golden age in the air at a public meeting, I am no more than a spectator of other men's and women's work in the creation of this new star. I suspect myself of saying this in order to clear my conscience. I can usually do that by a series of sounding arguments. Otherwise I should not be able to enjoy my meals. Happily, there are plenty of other people whose consciences are less easily persuaded. I like meeting them and I should like to vote for them, but I can see no possibility of working with them so long as I have an argument left.

XIV. *On Being Cruel*

A KINDLY censor has levelled a charge of excessive kindliness against me. It is a strange fact that nothing puts an ordinary human being on his defence more quickly than to have one of the virtues imputed to him. Who except a Prime Minister would not be insulted by being described as a "good, honest man"? Authors tear their hair if reviewers say that their books are "readable." Schoolboys, if they are still the same as they were a generation ago, resent any suspicion that they are "hard-working." Ruskin scribbled furious footnotes against critics who declared that he wrote beautifully. Lamb became irritated when Coleridge referred to him as "gentle." There are, it is said, virtuous young men who, if anyone calls them "virtuous," will lie like Peter as if in contradiction of a calumny. Soldiers, who are acclaimed as "heroes," assure us earnestly that they are nothing of the sort, but either that they only did what anybody else would have done in the same circumstances or that what seemed a brave action was the result of losing their heads through fright. There is scarcely any kind of merit, indeed, that a man will not disown if he is publicly saddled with it. No man likes to be called "sober" or "pious" or "modest" or "practical" or "sane." There is a famous hymn, "Ashamed to be a Christian," which makes it evident that even Christians have been known to deny their Christianity in public. It used to be told of Robert Browning that, when someone asked him in public if he was a Christian, he thundered "No." It is a widespread human instinct to reply "No," frequently even when we do not mean it. Scott went so far as to reply "No" when he was asked whether he was the author of *Waverley*. The motives for saying "No" are, of course, various. The soldier who wins the Victoria Cross and is called a hero says "No," as a rule, out of modesty. Scott said "No" because he felt that nobody had the right to pry into his secrets. Ruskin said "No," when he was praised for his writing, because he knew that the critics preferred his writing to his thinking. In the same way, most men who are described as "honest," "sober," "industrious" and "modest" are resentful because they feel that the praise of these qualities conveys an insinuation that they are lacking in other and more star-like qualities. The schoolboy would rather you believed he had won a scholarship through cleverness than through hard work, for there is more satisfaction to his vanity in the thought that he is clever. Let him take to writing in later life, however, and he will acquire a distaste for being called "clever"; he will feel that those who are calling him "clever" are denying him the one infinitely precious thing, genius. Human beings are suspicious of most praise, indeed,

On Being Cruel

not because it is excessive, but because by its very definiteness it seems to set a limit on the good things that can be said of them. Not until they die do they quite abandon the hope of being praised for qualities that they know in their secret hearts they do not possess. How happy I felt many years ago when I heard that a man—who had met me only once, be it said, and that for a few moments in the shadows round a street-lamp—had described me as a "tall, athletic-looking chap like a Spanish sailor"! I do not think he had ever seen a Spanish sailor, but the praise, in that it flattered my secret wishes, was good.

On the whole, however, I fancy that if I had been present I should have said "No" even to this. There is a luxury in mere contradiction—in telling someone that he is wrong. That is what the Americans call a natural "reaction" with many of us. (An American who inscribed a copy of his new book to me the other day concluded with the words: "Would appreciate your reactions.") I know that on being described as "kindly," my first reaction was to sit down and prove to myself, if to nobody else, that I was nothing of the sort. I recalled with a glow of pleasure the occasion on which I had been called "rancorous" on account of something I had written about Mr. Kipling. I rejoiced in the nine times I had been accused of political venom. I blessed the critic who had said that, under a mask of sweet reasonableness, I was full of hatred and all uncharitableness. As for the man on the provincial weekly, who denounced

The Peal of Bells

me for poisoning the wells of truth, I hoped, as I thought of him, that his salary had since been doubled. I felt a heavy debt of gratitude to the man who said that I "wielded the rapier rather than the bludgeon," and an equally heavy debt of gratitude to the other man who said that I "wielded the bludgeon rather than the rapier." Accusation after accusation of malice, bitterness, and brutality swept back from the past into my memory, sweet as a stream of honey. In the mirror of self-flattery, I saw an image of myself as an exquisitely monstrous creature, red in tooth and claw, solitary and cruel as a hawk. Then I began to rewrite in my mind all that I had ever written about human beings or birds so as to wring all the alleged kindliness out of it and to leave it with the livelier flavour of savagery. Unfortunately, human beings do not lend themselves to savage treatment, when one is writing about them. I do not say that they are all lovable, but most of them are quite likeable if you do not see too much of them. They are so good-natured, so obliging, and, in nine cases out of ten, they work so very hard for so small a return. Precipitated, without being consulted so far as one knows, on to an exceedingly dangerous and unsteady planet, they find themselves almost as soon as they have left school confronted with problems that are as far beyond their powers of solution as the squaring of the circle. They do not know why they are here or where they will be next. They do not know whether they are at the

On Being Cruel

beginning of things or at the end of things—whether the world in which they and their children are passengers is on the road to ruin or is rapidly approaching the delightful gates of Paradise. They have no security of health or life or money. To-morrow is an unknown country, and all that they know is that, if they live they will visit it, and that after that they will never visit it again. They practise a heroic make-believe that all is well and even that all is permanently well, and the head of a great business or a host at a dinner-party behaves as though he were an immortal. Time stands still in presence of his happiness and success; and death, if it is mentioned, is only a theme for a jest—a fabulous hypothesis. All the time, his future is as precarious as a sparrow's, and his problems are in great measure the same as the sparrow's—how to remain alive on this mortality-haunted ball of mud and water and how to feed his young so that they, too, may be able in time to solve the difficult problem of how to remain more or less comfortably alive till they die. Domestic animals, it is true, have these problems solved for them—though not, perhaps, in the most satisfactory manner; but the wild creatures, of whom man is chief, live in the wildernesses of chance, and, if a man has the gift of thought, it is but another means of being anxious as to what is going to happen next to him and to his brood.

It seems to me impossible, as soon as one begins to reflect at all, not to pity this insignificant and bewildered creature who, to add to his troubles, has also an uneasy suspicion that he possesses an immortal soul. He has not much time, in the intervals of obtaining food, keeping warm, and enjoying the few and monotonous pleasures of life, to attend to his immortal soul, but how dreadful must his anxiety be when he is faced by the problem of how to keep alive not only in one world but in two! You could not possibly be unkind to him in such circumstances. It would be like throwing stones at a mourner at a funeral. I suspect, indeed, that most of the writers who have been cruel to the animal called man have been cruel through mischief. It is their fun and relaxation. Even Swift was savage only with his pen, and was as mild as milk when he met a helpless human being in the flesh. To-day there is a fashion of cruelty in writing, but its purpose is decoration, not interpretation. It takes life and makes it more grotesque than it is. Thus, in a great deal of fiction, we see men and women made as hideous as marionettes, and we do not mind how cruelly they are treated because nobody above a child of nine is offended by cruelty to a doll. But I doubt if you can paint a very cruel picture of human beings without being false to your models. You may hate your landlady while you are eating the breakfast she has served, but there is no use pretending that she is a crooked old murderess with rapacious claws who picks your pockets while you are in the bathroom and puts spirits of salt into your tea. You may say

On Being Cruel

many violent things—after she has left the room—when you take the first sip of her vile tea, but, when you see her in perspective against the background of the universe, you know that she is really a harmless, ignorant, and permanently tired animal who is doing her best to save enough money for her funeral. Then, if you are writing about children, what room is there for malice? You may make them ugly, but they are not. You may use your acids to eat away their pretty skins and to ruin their features, and, if you refer to a pretty child, you may mention only that it has no front teeth. You may even pretend that children are wicked, but then you will be in danger of becoming a psycho-analyst. You may re-write "Mary had a little lamb" in such a way as to suggest that Mary had originally stolen the lamb, that she enjoys nothing so much as beating it when she is alone with it in the back-garden, and that she is looking hungrily forward to the day on which it will be killed, and she will be able to get her teeth into a fine juicy chop. But all this would merely be libelling Mary; and the game of libelling Mary, though no doubt it is a good game, is no more serious a game than Mah Jongg. Similarly, if we are writing about birds, it is almost impossible not to feel fairly good-natured about them, and, if we tell malicious stories about them, it is only for fun. I am told that it is the modern fashion to speak ill of the robin and to paint him as the bird that murders his father. I am all in favour of telling the truth about the robin; but it should always be remembered that, even if he does murder his father, he does it only once. And he never seems to do it when you and I are looking. In fact, there is no bird that is more well-behaved in the presence of human beings. If all murderers were as charming, we should begin to doubt the iniquity of murder. And even when we see a really wicked-looking bird like a hawk killing and devouring its prey, do we feel censorious? Do we not tell ourselves that it knows no better and, in fact, that it has no alternative if it is to remain alive? But, if we are mild in our attitude to hawks, why not in our attitude to human beings? They, too, are driven by hunger, and the wickedness even of the worst of them does not continue much above three-score years and ten.

XV. *Puzzles*

YOU would think that life is full enough of puzzles—how to make both ends meet, how to get up in the morning when you are called, how to reconcile your conduct with your theories, how to pay compliments without telling lies—to satisfy any but an abnormal craving for difficulty. Yet man is hardly out of the cradle when he first begins to bewilder his brains with conundrums and riddle-me-rees; and he is still poring over the chess-problem in the morning paper within two steps of the grave. A learned man confessed to me that the reason why he buys one particular Sunday paper rather than another is that it contains the best acrostics, and, indeed, that the acrostic is usually all that he reads. I have no notion how many men and women are slaves to this pernicious and wasteful habit. It is, I fear, widespread, and we can but grieve that so many men of obviously exceptional intellect should be giving to acrostics what is meant for mankind. Persons of average brain-power quail before these worse than Sphinx's riddles. If we were sentenced to hard labour and given our choice between picking oakum as our daily task and reducing a length of this rhymed gibberish to reason, many of

The Peal of Bells

us would declare for picking oakum. Of all forms of verse, whether free or the kind that jingles its chains, the acrostic is the most maddening. I seldom read beyond the first four lines, which generally run something like this:

1. I am a plate, but not a plate.
2. Here King Cophetua sits in state.
3. Though strong, I end in weakest tea.
4. So is the word in front of me.

At this point I cease reading, not only in despair, but in disgust. Then, if by some horrible fascination I am impelled to turn to the same page on the following Sunday, I discover that the solution of the third line is the French word "Fort," and of the fourth line the word "Some," and that somehow or other the initial letters of the acrostic spell "Shelley," and the last letters "Dickens." Was there ever a smaller reward for such Herculean labour? If the mountain had actually enjoyed bringing forth the mouse, that would not have been more absurd than the satisfaction of men and women of intellect in solving an acrostic.

Yet we must not be too censorious. There are few of us who have never succumbed to the temptation of the puzzle, at least in its more innocent forms. It is not for me, indeed, of all men to throw stones, for my own first printed attempt at literature was a riddle-me-ree, that appeared in the columns of a religious paper called the *Witness,* when I was a child

Puzzles

of seven or eight. I do not remember exactly how it ran, but riddle-me-rees are all on the same pattern—something like:

> My *first* is in carrot, but not in bean;
> My *second* is in bishop, but not in queen;

and so on. I do remember, on the other hand, how much I enjoyed seeing my name in print, and how I was embarrassed with delight when an old gentleman with a beard came over to the pew after the morning service on the following Sunday and, as he shook hands with me warmly, whispered that he had solved my riddle-me-ree with a great deal of difficulty. There are people who speak as though sorrow and song were inseparable companions in the literary life, but I can assure you that, however true this may be of other poets, it is not true at all of the writers of riddle-me-rees. I can remember no emotions save those of pleasure connected with those first excursions on the lower slopes of Parnassus. Goaded by the love of fame, I now began to try my skill on anagrams, metagrams, and another kind of puzzle called decapitations; and I never became tired of seeing them in print with the author's name and age (in brackets) attached—thus: Y. Y. [aged 7¾]. My first literary jealousy was directed against a little girl who contributed a puzzle one week and gave her age as about a year less than my own. After that, my ambition began to soar in search of new conquests, and I turned my eyes hopefully to-

The Peal of Bells

wards London, saying to myself, "If I can get into the *Witness,* why not into *Little Folks?*" Alas for the grandiose dreams of mortals! Humiliation alone awaited me, and as I opened the magazine month after month, and turned to the puzzle page and found that no laboured light lines of mine had gained admission, I was initiated into the heartache of vanity in defeat. Ultimately, I accepted the verdict of London and abandoned the puzzle as an art-form, not without bitterness. Who knows but that my present hostility to acrostics is merely the spleen of a frustrated composer of riddles?

In spite of their painful associations, however, and though I ceased to take a professional interest in them, I did not permit myself to sink into misanthropic hatred of riddles in private life. I could still enjoy a puzzle or conundrum as much as anybody, and even at the present day I never see in print the lines beginning:

> As I was going to St. Ives,
> I met a man with seven wives

without a keen sense of pleasure, and of curiosity as to the answer. Nor, if I live to be a hundred, shall I ever cease to regard, with positive affection, that other admirable puzzle about the herring and a half that cost three-halfpence. If I had a tomb like Tutankhamen's, I should instruct my executors to make a copy of that conundrum on parchment, and leave it beside my mummy in a sealed bottle to amuse the

Puzzles

little children of three thousand years hence. But, perhaps, there is no need to take special pains to secure the future existence of such a trifle. If a man were as sure of immortality as the herring in the conundrum, what a load of care and apprehension would be lifted from the spirits of humanity! It is strange that a riddle that is only a sum in arithmetic should have won for itself in this fashion a place apart from all other sums. It differs only in memorableness, indeed, from those other sums beginning: "If 3 men working 8 hours a day gather 2 cwt. of apples . . ."

Perhaps the great charm of a riddle as compared with an ordinary sum is that it looks as though it depended for its solution less on work than on guessing. Man is born under a compulsion to guess. He feels instinctively that that is his particular task in the universe. He discovered America and the art of flying by guessing. At least, he guessed first and proved his guesses afterwards. His religions are guesses in behalf of which nations have laid each other waste and timid girls have given their lives bravely. The finer part of his politics is a guess: had he never guessed but relied altogether on what he knew, he would never have advanced beyond the Bushman. His philosophies and arts are guesswork at secrets that will never be wholly revealed under the sun and moon; that is why philosophy and art can never exhaust themselves—there will always be the conflict between guess and guess. We sometimes treat our guesses as certainties, as when we go after a new theory such as that of the psycho-analysts, but a later age as often as not comes to the conclusion that our guess was wrong, and it guesses again, and again mistakes its guess for a certainty. Our very estimates of the characters, whether of dead or of living men, are guesses: we are still unable to agree about even such conspicuous figures as Marcus Aurelius and Napoleon. I do not mean to deny the existence of knowledge, but we have little enough knowledge either in religion or in philosophy, either in history or in medicine, either in æsthetics or in psychology, that does not leave us with a vast scope for guessing. Hence it is not strange that we like to practise guessing even in our games. There have never been any competitions in the papers that have been more popular than those that depended on guessing—guessing a missing word, or the leading football teams, or the first three horses in the Derby, or the results of a General Election. An element of skill, no doubt, enters into all these competitions, but, in choosing the winner of a horse-race and in similar matters, a good guess may beat all the skill and all the special knowledge in the world. A riddle, indeed, is a race in which knowledge is the tortoise and a guess is the hare, and the hare very often defies the fable and wins. I do not deny that the universal passion for guessing has been greatly stimulated by the fact that in the modern world a good guess is rewarded far beyond any other kind of

Puzzles

good work. Guess the winner of the Royal Hunt Cup and you will easily make twenty pounds: sit at a desk all day, on the other hand, adding up long columns of figures—a task for intellectual giants—and you will be paid only at the rate of the ordinary clerk. Even as a child, I am afraid, I enjoyed guessing all the more if there was an expectation of money with the answer. I remember with especial kindness a guessing game that a tall, grey-haired lady from Scotland—a third or fourth cousin—used to make us play when she came to the house. She would place half a crown in one of her hands and a two-shilling piece in the other, and would then put her hands behind her back, changing the coins from one to the other several times, and repeat the lines:

> Neevy neevy nick nack,
> Which hand will you tik tak?
> The right or the left
> Whichever you like best.

It was a glorious victory if one chose the hand that held the half-crown, but what an angel she was to have so substantial a consolation prize in the other hand for anyone who guessed wrong!

Let us not conclude, however, that all children are mere mercenaries in their love of guessing. They do not answer conundrums for money, nor are they the richer in pocket for guessing whom they have caught in a game of blind man's bluff or the solution of a charade. If children did not love guessing and

The Peal of Bells

making other people guess, they would not for ever be acting in charades in preference to all other kinds of play. How they beam like gods and goddesses of victory when at the end of the charade the riddle is unread and the audience has to "give it up"! Not, indeed, that all children who act in charades prefer the guessing part to the drama. I found myself lately in company that was almost indifferent to anything but the acting. It was in vain that I tried to get them to choose a word, and, indeed, looked up the dictionary in search of a difficult one, where I could find only unactable words like "palæontology" and "heliotherapy." "Don't let's trouble about the word yet," said a tall, dark girl, picking among the costumes; "let's make up the plot, and we'll think of the word afterwards. Shall we pretend that the house is on fire and that there's an old mad woman lying in bed and a ghost comes in——" A small boy with bright eyes caught her by the arm and interrupted her. "Shall I be the old mad woman lying in bed," he asked eagerly, "and give a fearful scream?" "What shall I be? What shall I be?" a mite of a girl, little more than a baby, kept appealing, dancing up and down with excitement. "Oh, you can be frightened of the ghost," the tall girl told her, "and scream, too." In the end we fixed on "rowdy" as the word, and those children certainly acted the first syllable to the life. So many of the actors were given no instructions but to be frightened and scream, and they carried out their instructions with such enthusiasm that I am afraid very little of the dialogue was audible to the audience. This seemed to me to be a corruption of the true spirit of charade, the chief object of which should be to set an insoluble puzzle to the onlookers. Not that I did not sympathize with the little boy who wanted to be an old mad woman lying in bed and give a fearful scream. I should have rather liked to play the part myself. But surely these joys can be combined with the profounder pleasures of the puzzle. It is delightful to be allowed to scream in a drawing-room, but it is still more delightful to hear the drawing-room echoing with the secretly bitter applause of people who have had to "give it up."

XVI. *The Christmas Present*

IT is a good rule to give a child what it asks for at Christmas, but I sympathized with the parents who were adamant when their small daughter was invited to choose her present and whispered, "An electric fruit dish." At the same time, I could almost see that electric fruit dish through the desirous eyes of the child, and I began to long to see it in the middle of the table. Not that I had ever cared for such things when I saw them in the shop windows. An illuminated glass apple is not really half so pretty as a real apple, and an illuminated glass pear has always seemed to me to be a dull libel on one of the most tempting of the fruits. Still, if I had been brought up in an electrical age, I feel sure that I also should have thought a make-believe pear in a shop window perfectly delicious, and that I should almost have preferred the lighted simulacra of grapes and oranges to any fruits that ever grew on vine or tree. The love of make-believe begins early, and is, perhaps, the parent of all the arts. It may have its origin in some instinctive doubt whether the things that we see are real, and in the feeling that, God having created this immense and populous illusion we call the earth, we, too, may as well become creators on our own account and people the

The Christmas Present

world with illusions that shall be the rivals of God's creatures. In this mood a child can make a baby out of a pocket-handkerchief and lavish on it a wealth of love that would make any human baby lie on its back and crow. There is no need for any vulgar likeness to life in these nursery imitations. The child creates its own little world, and, however grotesque it may seem to older eyes, it sees that it is all very good. Not that—in a comfortable home—it makes its own toys, but that it makes the beauty of them; and the rag doll with the dirty face and one eye missing and the straw visible through the hole in her crown, whom the little girl puts to bed with such tender admonitions, is a lovely and lovable creature whom grown-up eyes simply do not behold. Who shall say that the child is not wise in this passion for something born outside the circle of created things? Wise men in the East have told us that the world we live in is all a dream, and that we shall begin to see reality only when we understand that the things about us are unreal. Plato held the opinion that the things we see are but faulty copies of realities that exist in heaven, and it seems to follow that men and women are little more than dolls engaged in a game the explanation of which is in another world. Hence, the child's doll may be no further removed from a human being than human beings are removed from their counterparts in heaven. The child, if it were a philosopher, might say to us: "There is your world, and here is mine.

The Peal of Bells

Each of them is a toy, and a scene of toys. We are both for the moment taking them extremely seriously, but, whereas I shall escape from my illusion when I reach my 'teens, you will not escape from yours till you are dead. You laugh at me because I am so absorbed in make-believe, but you do not laugh at yourselves, though you are equally absorbed in make-believe. Things are important to you only in so far as you imagine them important, and the very house in which you live so happily and with such a sense of permanence is only a temporary toy which, in comparison even with so temporary a thing as the sun, is hardly more substantial or more lasting than a shadow. You, no more than I, have found the key to what is permanent, but live seriously in a world of playthings."

It is fortunate that children do not talk like this. But, if they did, after having sent them to a boarding-school to have the nonsense knocked out of them, we should have to admit that there was something in what they said. Having done so, we should also realize, perhaps, that the child, far from presenting the case against toys, had given us a strong argument for a greater use of toys than ever. We might possibly be driven to the conclusion that it would be well to escape from the conventional make-believe in which we live and venture among new make-believes which may, after all, be guesses at reality. Imaginative art is such a make-believe, and in its greatest periods has always presented us with a mimic world

The Christmas Present

that is more desirable than the world in which we live. Great plays are but noble puppet-shows, and great pictures the portraits of divine dolls. Shakespeare did not describe a world that can be found anywhere else outside the plays of Shakespeare, and Fra Angelico did not portray a Holy Family over whose lodging any eastern star had ever hung. Realists have come since and have attempted to put accurate copies of human beings into books and plays and pictures, and artists have even gone to Palestine in order to paint Mary and Joseph as life-like Jews in a life-like Jewish stable. These things are interesting, but great art has other business than to make believe that the make-believe of common life is true. It must resemble nature in some measure; even the doll made from a handkerchief must have some visible division into a head and a body. A child might be able to pretend that a walking-stick was a baby, but it could not pretend that a pair of boots or a teapot was a baby. Its happiness in its toy, however, as has been said, does not depend on its being a clever and close copy of something else, but in the magical investment of the imagination. Had Zola gone to the nursery, he might have realized why his painstaking reports on the lives of men and women were of trivial significance beside the *Midsummer Night's Dream* with its make-believe fools and fairies. It is possible, and, indeed, probable, that the incredible story of Cinderella will outlive all the painfully credible novels of the nineteenth-century

The Peal of Bells

realists. For the author of *Cinderella* had been given the key to the freedom of make-believe, while the realists thought that they were serving reality in turning themselves into slavish copyists. I fancy the parents who objected to giving the child the electric fruit dish did so chiefly, not because the fruit was so unlike real fruit, but because it was meant to be too near and cunning an imitation of it. The child did not mind this, for a child likes for its own sake almost anything that is made in imitation of something in the common world. It likes a piece of chocolate that pretends to be a cigarette or a cigar, or a piece of marzipan coloured to look like a strawberry. It likes a piece of wood that looks more or less like a cow, or a piece of wood that looks more or less like Noah the great sailor. It likes a piece of metal or stuffed leather that is made in the image of the beasts of the forest or the birds of the air. All it asks is that, besides the everyday world in which its parents are emperor and empress, it shall be allowed to enjoy this second world of make-believe, in which make-believe legs of mutton are cooked in a make-believe stove and served on make-believe plates at a make-believe table surrounded by make-believe chairs. It claims the right to create its own simular world, and, if its parents will not or cannot provide it with the materials for doing so, it will do so itself, as E. Nesbit showed some years ago, out of cardboard and rags and old medicine bottles. A child, indeed, can create a very fine apple out of a breath of air, and

The Christmas Present

we have all seen children in the nursery, without making use of a single toy, sitting round an invisible table, raising invisible spoons to their mouths, and tasting the deliciousness of invisible foods.

We, too, may as well admit that, when we become serious and let our thoughts wander outside our own tiny and rascally lives, we are even as the children. The history of the universe is for us the history of a toy. Intellectually, we may be evolutionists and all sorts of things, but in our imaginations God hangs the sun and the moon in the sky as one hangs knick-knacks on a Christmas tree. The creation of the world is for most of us like the replenishing of a wonderful toy-cupboard. The fishes and the creeping things and the beasts of the field—why, one has had them made of celluloid and seen them floating in the bath! Later came the fall of man through eating an apple that might have been found in the toe of a Christmas stocking. The redemption of man is once more a scene of toys, and the ox and the ass that before him bow are inhabitants not of a farm but of a nursery. This does not prove that we are frivolous. The men who painted these things most beautifully for us—Fra Angelico and Fra Lippo Lippi—were both monks, and it was only in the days of irreligion that men began to paint the manger as a manger would appear to everyday eyes. The toy does not belittle but heightens the wonder of life. No man has ever loved an ox or an ass who has not loved the invented image of it, and it is only

The Peal of Bells

when they become playthings of the imagination that they seem the perfect company for the divine infant. The wise men and the shepherds and the star—these are not to be found in the annals but only in the imagination childishly creating a lovelier story than is to be found in history. I do not mean that the story is untrue. I am sure the paintings of Fra Angelico are true in a far profounder sense than the writings of Tacitus or Josephus. The painters of the golden background saw past the facts of life and realized that beyond the make-believe of to-day and yesterday is a divine play that can still be represented in dolls and Christmas toys. Were I a philosopher, I should write a philosophy of toys, showing that nothing else in life need be taken seriously, and that Christmas Day in the company of children is one of the few occasions on which men become entirely alive. Certainly the writer, whether poet or historian, who cannot fill his scene with puppets and painted birds is a mere mouther of wind who can make on us no impression of reality. Let him buy an electric fruit dish and meditate on its marvels.

XVII. *School*

SCHOOL, on the whole, cuts a poor figure in literature. Lamb and Dickens, the humanest of all those who have written on it, depict its miseries rather than its joys. School in their pages is a penal settlement—the purgatory of lonely and sensitive boys. If reformatories were conducted in such a manner nowadays, there would be an outcry against them. The belief that learning can be whacked into a boy through the palm of the hand or the breeches scarcely exists any longer except among the Sadists.

I am no authority on the older type of school, for I have never seen a cane used in my life. Other boys from other schools used to relate their experiences with plagose headmasters and describe how, by laying a hair from a horse's tail across your palm, you could outwit or at least diminish the sting of the cane. I do not know whether the belief in the horsehair had any foundation. I only know that I had but to picture a boy, weaponless save for an invisible hair, affronting an angry schoolmaster, in order to admire him above Ulysses. School was for me, however, a place free from bodily perils ever since the day on which, at the age of five, I was taken to a kindergarten run by two German ladies and asked

The Peal of Bells

to read out something about a spider from a *Nelson's Royal Reader,* so that it might be seen for what class I was fitted. How much seemed to depend upon my effort! It was the first public test to which I had ever been put, and I do not know whether I came through it with credit or not. I was like a chicken that had broken through its shell into the daze of a new world. Cortes on seeing the Pacific for the first time may have felt as I did. Everything was at once as strange and clear as in a dream, but even in a dream I had never seen such faces or heard such voices as the kindly faces and voices of the Frau and the Fräulein. I do not think I either liked or disliked the notion of going to school. I merely resigned myself philosophically to the doom of all children. I did not like standing in a crowd of children round the piano singing hymns, and I did not care for playing games on the bare floor under the eye of a schoolmistress, but I liked to sit and look at pictures of dogs and horses while Fräulein Fenkohl touched them with a pointer and made us repeat after her "Der Hund" and "Das Pferd." If I hated the German songs we were taught, it was only because at home I was constantly being cajoled into singing them to visitors. Hence the sulky expression that has brooded over my face till the present day. My vividest memory of the kindergarten, however, is of nothing I learned there, but of a day on which the nurse called for us early and took us off home because a mad bull had been

School

shot in the street in which we lived. It seems to me, as I look back on it, curiously illogical to have hurried us off home in this fashion, now that the bull was dead. But it was not every day that a mad bull was shot in Elmwood Avenue, and, amid the excitement, I suspect, no one at home could believe in our safety till they had the evidence of their eyes that we were alive. What made the incident all the more real to our imaginations was the fact that the bull belonged to our butcher. Some days afterwards, when I went round the shops with my mother, we called at the butcher's to order a sirloin. When she was ordering it, I tugged at her sleeve till she stooped down to listen to me. "Yes, dear," she said, "what is it?" "Tell him, not from the mad bull," I told her earnestly. She laughed and passed on my request to the butcher, and the butcher laughed. He gave me his promise, however, and assured me that he wouldn't dream of sending a joint from the mad bull to our house. But, if I shrank from contact with mad bulls dead, it was nothing to the way in which I began to shrink from them while they were still alive. I went about for a time in almost as great dread of mad bulls as of Papists. Every bullock that was being driven to market along the road was for some time afterwards a potential mad bull in my eyes, and a herd of bullocks a potential herd of mad bulls. One day, on my way to school, I saw twenty or thirty bullocks advancing along the road from the opposite direction with confused and low, ered heads. Fearing that my last day had come, I rushed up to an old gentleman, thrust my hand into his overcoat pocket, and looking up into his face, shouted, "Mad bulls! mad bulls!" at the top of my voice. Poor man, he stared down at me with the utmost perplexity. He possibly thought that he was being assaulted by a mad child, but before he could gather his wits to speak, the cattle had swept past, and, sure of my safety, I had broken away and was running off up the road, and, at the end of a few seconds, was laughing at my memory of the old gentleman, as though it were he and not I who had cut the absurd figure. You will see, however, that going to a somewhat distant kindergarten was an experience more exciting than was, perhaps, altogether suitable to a tiny and timid boy. If I had stayed on at it, I should undoubtedly have developed into an athlete, for no child of five ever learned to sprint faster at the sight of a cow. Still, I was not sorry at the end of a year to be taken away and sent to a more arduous school that was only a few doors away from us.

How delightful is the introduction to all one's new books at the beginning of a new school-year! Some men tell us that they never outlive their sense of excitement on seeing the curtain go up at the beginning of a play. The child, I think, feels something like the same excitement on taking a new school-book into its hands. Later on, it may come to regard it with indifference or even with aversion,

School

but who can turn the unsullied pages of a new schoolbook without an exquisite premonitory joy? One's pleasure is mainly the pleasure of curiosity. Here are new, strange territories in which one must travel. Or, it might be nearer the mark to say, here are rooms in the new, strange house in which one is going for a year to live. Even a cat enjoys going into a room that it has never seen before and that has just been unlocked. How much more does a child enjoy the first sight and touch of a new book! *Little Arthur's History of England, Sullivan's Spelling-Book Superseded, Harbinson's Geography*—they are not, perhaps, the books that one would pray to be left alone with on a desert island, but once for a few days they represented the unexplored world, and we did not stay to ask whether the world was worth exploring. It may be that from the outset there is an instinctive thirst for knowledge in us, and that this early appetence deludes us into unwarrantable hopes at the sight even of a new geography. If so, it is not long before we are disenchanted, and the more we learn of the exports of foreign countries and of the dates and the wives of kings, the less highly we esteem them. There is little enough of this knowledge that we would acquire save under compulsion. Still, I do not think we ever abandon hope entirely, but, as we are betrayed into disappointment at one stage of a subject after another, we look forward with all the more eagerness to the next. Thus it was in arithmetic. Multiplication might be vexation, and division dullness, but how ardently we went on to proportion! How thrilling was our introduction to practice (a branch of arithmetic of which, alas, I remember nothing but the name)! I looked up the word in the dictionary to-day, but that did not help me. According to my dictionary, practice is "a rule or method in arithmetic to facilitate multiplying qualities in different denominations." How like an English translation of Hegel! Yet this was one of the tasks that were set to us as little children. Greatly did I prefer spelling. As this is now generally regarded as a low accomplishment, I may say, without boasting, that I was very good at it. Yet it is odd that the only word I remember spelling in the schoolroom was one that I failed to spell correctly. "Creature," said the schoolmistress when it came to my turn. "C-r double-e c-h-e-r," I answered. "No, no," she said, "not creecher—creature, an animal." I again misheard the word, and saw in my mind's eye a little crawling insect, called a "creecher," of which I had never before heard; and, obstinate as the child in Wordsworth, I repeated: "C-r double-e c-h-e-r." I was vexed with myself when the next boy answered and I realized that the word was "creature," which I could have spelt, so to speak, in my sleep. It is a curious fact that, when we look back on our childhood, nothing stands out more clearly than our most trivial mistakes. I remember nothing of the reading class except being corrected one day for pronouncing "de-

School

termined" "detterminded." I remember nothing of those readings from the Bible with which we always began Monday's school except that a little fair-haired girl, whose turn it was to read the verse about the suicide of Judas Iscariot: "And all his bowels gushed out," pronounced the first syllable of "bowels" as thought it rhymed with "go." I can scarcely remember, indeed, whether I cared for any of the subjects we were taught in those early years. I remember much more clearly the pleasure I took in the patterns of the covers of new exercise-books—patterns like the veinings in marble. The first subject, I think, from which I got a definite and entrancing pleasure was Latin. This may have been partly because it was the first subject I was taught by a master, and so seemed to advance me a stage in manhood. But I think I loved the language for its own sake, and enjoyed declining *"mensa,* a table" and *"puer,* a boy" with a novitiate delight in the ever-delightful game of words. Latin grammar, they say, is a dry subject. I never found it so. There is a pleasure of mastery—of a continuously increasing mastery of a precise and clearly-marked world—to be had from it, such as the mathematical child may obtain from Euclid, but that I, at least, could never obtain from the incoherent facts of history or geography. It was in the Latin class, too, in that admirable work, *Fabulæ Faciles,* that I first read of the labours of Hercules and of the quest of the Golden Fleece and realized that there were other stories almost as good as "Jack the Giant-Killer" and Hans Andersen's "Ugly Duckling." *Fabulæ Faciles* is the only book of the time of which the charm did not fade as the pages became soiled with use. Even *Fabulæ Faciles* did not persuade me that it was better to go to school than to stay away from it. But, if I had to go to school, here at least was a reward for my pains.

Even more, perhaps, was it a reward, when school was over, to cross the road to the cinder-path under the limes and to take part in the rush of the game of Wild Boar. How enviable seemed those powerful or slippery boys who had a genius for eluding the hands of captors—for casting them off, indeed, as a rock throws back the tide! For myself, I was as a rule an early capture, with tentacles of arms flung around me while the fatal formula, "One, two, three, a man for me, lock him!" was gibbered as if in a single breath. But it was pleasant to mingle, even as an incompetent, with such heroes. I have always enjoyed the company of heroes indeed almost as much as I should enjoy being a hero myself. I first tasted this pleasure when playing Wild Boar after school. I can still taste it to-day. Perhaps it is for this reason more than for any other that my schooldays shed a golden light through the chambers of my memory.

XVIII. *On Going to Scotland*

IT was very dark and, naturally, it was raining, as the train crossed the border at, I think, a station called Berwick. It was impossible to see anything through the dining-car windows except the streams running down the panes and the blurred reflections of our own long illuminated box. Nevertheless I experienced a strange lifting of the heart as the train bore me on deeper and ever deeper into this wild, dark country that I had so often longed to visit. I had the pleasant emotions of a foreigner, to whom all places that the eye of Heaven doth visit are exciting or amusing. There was a little stern-browed man with a red moustache sitting at the table opposite to mine and pouring soda-water into a glass of whisky. It was with difficulty that I kept from addressing him in his own tongue: "Ha'ein' a wee yin, Sandy?" He wore such an earnest expression as he drank his whisky-and-soda, however, that I was not sure that he would take my well-meant raillery in good part. On the whole I concluded that, as Scotsmen are a sensitive race, the best thing I could do was to keep a chain on my lips and, indeed, not to speak to the natives until I was spoken to.

I began then to meditate on this unexpected craving of mine to call a respectable middle-aged Scots-

The Peal of Bells

man "Sandy." It is not, I told myself, that Scotsmen are anything new to me. I have known Scotsmen all my life, and I have never either known any of them to be called "Sandy" or even wished to call one of them "Sandy" before. Yet here in their own country I realized that I felt differently towards them. I was like Broadbent in Ireland. Harry Lauder tunes began to lilt back up the laneways of my memory—old songs, too, about "bonny lassies" and "juist a drappie in oor ee." I recalled from the days of my youth in Manchester one young Scotsman, with so sober an eye yet with so very little else that was sober about him, who at midnight used to make us join in the chorus of "Doon the burn, Davey lad," at one o'clock used very tenderly and very tearfully to make us join in the chorus of "Kind, kind and gentle is she," and at two o'clock in the morning, with sobs in his throat and his tumbler of whisky on the top of the piano, used to sing "All people that on earth do dwell." He was a very unfortunate young man. He belonged to a Presbyterian family, and was believed by his parents to be a teetotaller. Consequently, he never dared to go home till he was sure his father was asleep. His almost scared anxiety to spare his father's feelings was one of the most touching instances of filial devotion I have ever known. "No," he would say, pulling out his watch under a lamp at about half-past three, as we walked about the streets to keep him company, "the old fellow may be sitting up for me

On Going to Scotland

yet. I daren't risk it for another hour." And then, as he advanced, he bellowed at the top of his voice, so that all the stars and all Manchester could hear him: "'Tis the march, 'tis the march, 'tis the mar-r-r-ch of the Cameron men." It is always embarrassing to be in the company of a man who insists on drawing the attention of the police, especially if one does not know him very well. As a matter of fact, I scarcely knew this Scotsman except as his unwilling audience in the small hours. He was a young business man with an obscure passion for the company of journalists, whom, I fancy, he regarded with veneration as embodiments of the intellectual life. There was, unhappily, very little opportunity for the intellectual life while he was present, for, when he was not telling us how sad it was that he could never go home in the evenings for fear his family might notice his breath, he was usually roaring snatches of song about having "paidled in the burn" or about laying him doon and deeing for bonnie Annie Laurie or about "no being fou." However, he seemed to lead a charmed life. It may be that the police knew that, whatever his faults, he was a good son.

Even after more than twenty years his rendering of "All people that on earth do dwell" came back to me as I sat in the train that hurried me towards Glasgow. Not that I thought of him as a characteristic Scottish figure. Most of the Scotsmen I have known have been quiet men who did not sing in the street. They have, most of them, per-

The Peal of Bells

haps, been slightly addicted to "paidling in the burn" at smoking concerts, but they have been rather above than below the average in all the virtues that make for peace and prosperity in the home. Probably the Manchester Scot was brought back to my memory through association with the Harry Lauder tunes that kept running in my head to the accompaniment of the noise of the wheels of the train. It would have been in vain, however, to peer out through the wet windows in search of any such grotesque figure. Nowhere, at that hour, was anyone to be seen paidling in the burn in the darkness and the rain. Everybody in the dining-car itself looked depressingly normal. There was not an accent to be heard that I might not have heard in Fleet Street. Scotland, I confess, was at a first glance disappointing me—Scotland that I had never visited since the age of two.

By the age of two, I am told, I had been in Scotland three times, and it was in Scotland that I first learned to walk. Scotland, if the truth must be told, did not teach me to walk very well, but to be able to walk at all is something, and so far I feel that I am in Scotland's debt. I do not know whether I really remember anything of those early visits, but I persuade myself that I remember a steep street in Oban with a shop full of toys at the head of it and, in the countryside, shaggy cattle of a kind that I have never seen since except in an Academy picture. It will be seen, however, that, in revisiting Scotland

On Going to Scotland

after so long an interval, I was returning to a scene associated with one of the triumphs of my infancy. I am a Scotsman, I told myself, at least in my legs. And I have other sentimental links with Scotland. I used to hear a story, when I was a child—true or false, I do not know—that one of my ancestors was a Scottish Presbyterian minister who scandalized his parish by wearing silver buckles on his shoes and, as a means of getting rid of so undesirable a character, was sent as a missionary to the northern parts of Ireland. I have always been vain of those silver buckles. I also think of them with gratitude, because, if it had not been for them, my ancestor might never have left Scotland, and I might never have been born. I was thus, by the time the train was drawing into Edinburgh, in a mood to feel that I was arriving, after several generations' absence, in my native capital.

It was so much the more exasperating that all of it that I could see was a number of lamps in a dark railway-station. Here was I, for the first time in my life, in the loveliest city in this witch-shaped island, and I could see no more of it than if I had been sitting on the platform at Balham. There is, however, a curious and unjustifiable pleasure in passing even through the station of a city famous for its history or its beauty. How often have I sat in the train in Chester station and delighted in the quaint and ancient shop-fronts, though I could not see them, and had never seen them! So that I did not con-

The Peal of Bells

sider my visit to Edinburgh wasted. Why, it is pleasant to be told that one has once visited a famous town in one's childhood, even if one does not remember. It used to cause me considerable satisfaction to know that, as a baby, I had driven through Glasgow in a cab.

And now I was returning to Glasgow for the first time after all these derelict years. "Auld Reekie!" I murmured affectionately as I sat in the taxi and drove through its wet and night-filled streets. I am told, it is Edinburgh that is called "Auld Reekie," but I seldom know things of that sort until I have learned them by actually going to the place and reading the guide-book. When I got to the hotel, I immediately went to my room and a greying-haired chambermaid came along with me. I asked her if I might have a bath at half-past seven in the morning—I usually become rather irresponsible when I stay at hotels—and, when she had answered me, she looked at me curiously and said: "Yerr an Irish gentleman!" with the emphasis on the word "Irish." I agreed, and she inquired: "From the Orange pairts?" I assented again, but told her that I was not absolutely an Orangeman. "Ah'm a Protestant maself," she assured me, nodding gravely. I told her that I had friends of both persuasions. "Ma husband was a Catholic," she said, as though she were telling me a fact of extraordinary importance, "but ah'm a staunch Protestant." You who have never lived in Belfast can,

On Going to Scotland

perhaps, hardly understand how childishly happy it can make a Belfast man to be greeted with a conversation like this on arriving for the first time in a strange city. Outside Belfast it is almost impossible to find anybody who takes the slightest interest in one's religion, yet here was a sober-faced, middle-aged Scotswoman who had gone straight to the heart of the matter in five minutes. Nothing could have happened that would have made me feel more comfortably at home on my first night in Glasgow.

I do not know whether it is the custom in Glasgow to address all men as "gentleman"; but that is how the chambermaid always addressed me. "Here's your tea, gentleman," she would say, as she came in in the morning; or "Get up now, gentleman; it's half-past seven"; or "May I have a read of your *Herald*, gentleman, when you're done with it?" And her grave, friendly figure—she never smiled—would retreat leisurely through the door.

In spite of being spoken to in this unaccustomed fashion, and in spite of the mood in which I had crossed the border, I felt much less of a foreigner in Glasgow than I had expected to feel. Perhaps it was that the blood of the minister with the silver buckles knew that it was at last at home. I even admired the appearance of the city—its imposing four-square dignity in the rain—contrary to all I had ever heard of the place except from Glasgow men. If there must be towns in which people make money—and there is apparently no help for it—then

The Peal of Bells

I wish they could all be as handsome as Glasgow and Liverpool and Turin. But perhaps I see Glasgow through eyes that were too sentimental to be critical. To me it was undoubtedly the City of the Silver Shoe-buckles.

XIX. *The Collar*

IT is said that every man is both conservative and revolutionary. You may like novelty in politics and hate it in socks. The latest revolution in the dress of society may delight you as much as the latest revolution in the organization of society horrifies you. The women who are most conservative in their politics, indeed, are probably those who have the greatest passion for what is new in their clothes. There are, on the other hand, many persons like myself who would rather see changes political than changes sartorial. I do not remember any change in the fashions of men's dress that I liked on its first appearance. I temperamentally dislike even a new kind of collar. How I detested the double or "barmaid" collar when it was first introduced! Artists declared that it was a great improvement on the old high single collar that surrounded the neck like a white wall. But habit rather than beauty settled the matter for me, and I refused to make any concession on the point even to widespread public sentiment. Later on, men began to wear soft collars, and I still remained faithful to the old white wall. It was only when, after a friend's protests, I kept my eyes open one day during a walk through the streets to see what other men were wearing and could not find a single other person wearing the same kind of collar as myself, that I became alarmed lest I might be becoming an eccentric and resolved to fall in with the times. Some people have a notion that it is only dandies who have these troubles about their dress. There could not be a greater mistake. I am sure I have given as much thought to collars, hats, ties and boots as if I were the best-dressed man in London. When I changed from a stiff to a soft collar, it cost me a wrench such as a man must feel who crosses the floor in the House of Commons. I do not suppose it was any sentimental associations with stiff collars that caused this. It was simply that I was accustomed to think of myself as a person in a stiff collar, and I had a lazy dislike of having to accustom myself to a different-looking person in a soft one. Even vanity, which is the commonest infirmity in persons of my sex, had very little to say in the business. I honestly believe that in dress I am mainly guided by an indolent hostility to change. As soon as I began to wear a soft collar, I realized that it was both more comfortable and less ugly than its predecessor, and, within a few months, I had become as conservative in regard to it as I had previously been in regard to the other. When the War came to an end, and men went back to starch as to one of the blessings and symbols of peace, nothing but mockery in the streets could have induced me to follow the general fashion. To-day I still wear a soft collar, and wonder that human

The Collar

beings should ever have been content to wear any other kind. I shall probably go on doing so till one day, walking through the streets, I suddenly become aware that I am alone in my practice. On that day I, too, will go back to starch. I have no sufficient passion for any article of dress to be willing to look odd for the sake of wearing it.

In this I think I am a typical moderate Conservative. If everybody began to wear tall hats again, I should at first regard it as an outrage to be expected to do so. I should declare that I was free to wear what I pleased, and that never would I submit to such an indignity. I might even send a subscription to the Anti-Tall-Hat League. As time passed, however, and I saw my friends and acquaintances one by one accepting the new fashion as a matter of course and wearing tall hats without any noticeable alteration in their characters, my feelings would gradually change, and I should probably forget the next year to send in my subscription. Then I should suddenly realize to my horror that there were only about three of us left, and that I looked rather odd in a world that had gone over in chorus to the tall hat. I should then, rather shamefacedly, pay a visit to a hatter, and, when I found a silk hat to fit me, I should feel strangely pleased, and tell myself that it was not so uncomfortable after all, and that it suited me much better than I had expected. There is a peculiar pleasure to be had from looking like everybody else. What everybody else is wearing becomes in itself the standard of rightness, and, when once we have accepted it, we get from it a satisfaction comparable to that which we obtain from a good conscience. I do not know whether this is due to cowardice or to some positive social virtue. But I do know that, great as are the pleasures of being odd, the pleasures of not being odd rival and probably surpass them. Art-students in their 'teens, in revolt against everything that is prosaic and utilitarian, delight in challenging society with strange hats, strange bows, strange cloaks, strange costumes and strange collars; and it is an amusing game while it lasts. As men grow older, however, they feel less and less inclined to differentiate themselves from their fellows in so obvious a fashion, and put whatever art is in them into their work rather than into their personal appearance. They know before they are thirty that life is too short for a full-grown man to have time to waste on deliberately looking unlike his fellow-creatures. It is impossible to make any general rule on the subject that has not many exceptions; but it is safe to say that among elderly men those who set out with the most determined purpose to look like artists are nearly always those who are the least artistic in any achievement but their dress. The great artist, we may be sure, feels that dress is not a sufficiently important matter to make it worth a man's while to refuse to conform to the custom of his time in regard to it. He is

The Collar

more anxious to mix with his fellows as one of them than to walk among them as a bird of paradise for their comments and their stares.

Thus, though I hate new fashions in clothes, I believe that every sound argument is in favour of falling in with them. Our reluctance either to adopt them or not to adopt them is, I believe, almost entirely, a reluctance to look peculiar. I should feel very peculiar, for instance, if I wore spats, but I can imagine circumstances in which I should feel still more peculiar if I did not wear spats, and, after a struggle, I should begin to wear them. If I were permitted I should usually go on doing the thing that I had always done, and should make few concessions even to the seasons. I remember, when I was a boy, I seldom put on an overcoat till winter was half through. I had grown accustomed to summer, and I went on living as if it were summer, till long after everybody else had accepted the fact that the cold months were upon us. Similarly, when once I had put on an overcoat, I did not like taking it off again. I usually wore it even in the classroom, and it was only when there was not another overcoat to be seen under the blue sky of spring that I discarded it for the season. Not that I have not also experienced the pleasure of being the first as well as that of being the last—the first to wear a straw hat, the first to leave off the waistcoat during a blazing Easter. There is some gratification in being a pioneer even in so small a matter as this. Possibly there is the same gratification in being in advance of the crowd in recognizing some new author or artist. Here, however, as in regard to clothes, I yield to new fashions slowly, and find it even more of a struggle ultimately to conform. I find it difficult to believe that the world will ever again produce so good a poet as Shakespeare, so good a biographer as Johnson's Boswell, so good an essayist as Montaigne in one sort and Lamb in another. There are others, however, who seem rather to seek in literature for something that will satisfy their craving for novelty. Even if they become enthusiastic about an old author, it is usually about one who has become the novelty of the moment as a result of having been set on a new pedestal—some Donne or Webster. There is no means of deciding which of us gets the greater happiness from books. With most of us the pleasures are mingled—the pleasure in tradition and the pleasure in novelty. It is possible for the same man to enjoy both Milton and the Georgians. The chief difference between the lover of tradition and the lover of novelty is that the one will like a thing in spite of its being new, while the other will like it on account of its being new. It is, no doubt, fortunate for literature that there should be both kinds of readers—those who are so reluctant to admit that the good books to which they are accustomed can be equalled that they insist on a new book proving its right to enter the charmed circle, and those

The Collar

who are so eager to welcome what is new that they open the door alike to rubbish and to genius at the first knock.

This train of reflections began, as the essay itself began, with a collar. I was going out to dinner and, remembering that I was short of collars, I went into a shop to buy some. I asked for a wing collar, size 16, either 1¾ or 2¼ inches high—I could not remember which I wanted. The shopman brought out a box and showed me a number of collars with large Euclidian angles. "Haven't you any with round corners?" I asked him, for I had for years, when in evening dress, been wearing collars with wings like butterflies. I remember disliking them when they were first invented, but I had grown accustomed to them, and for that reason alone now preferred them to any other. "Haven't one in the shop," said the man behind the counter; "nobody wears them now, so they've stopped making them. This is the collar you want," he assured me; "it's a good collar"; and he took one out and showed me the name of the manufacturer. I have so little of an eye for costume that I confess I had not noticed that men were no longer wearing collars with butterfly wings, and I was rather suspicious of the shopman, for there was a large advertisement of a clearance sale in the window. However, I yielded to his persuasions, and bought a number of collars which I regarded with considerable hostility. When I got out into the street

The Peal of Bells

my hostility increased, and so great was my longing for my own sort of collar that within five minutes I found myself in another shop asking for "a wing collar with round wings, size 16, and 1¾ inches high," and I was elated when the shopman produced what I wanted without a moment's hesitation. At the same time, so strange is human nature that, as the result of what the previous shopman had said, I did not now quite like the look of the collar with the round wings. I bought it and went off home with both kinds, but, by the time I had begun to dress, the shopman's "Nobody wears them now" had sunk so effectively into my mind that it would have required an effort of will to put on the butterfly collar. The collar with square-angled wings began to assume a new charm as I thought that everybody was wearing it, and that on this point this evening everybody and I would be at one. I was still uncertain whether the shopman had spoken the truth, but it is difficult entirely to disbelieve a draper or a tailor, and undoubtedly the angular collar looked rather well. I set out for dinner not without a lingering doubt, but, when I arrived, a moment's glance told me that every other man present was wearing exactly the same sort of collar as myself, and I felt that peculiar joy of being dressed like everybody else which is known only to the civilized races. The worst of it is, I know I shall get fond of this shape of collar, and that other people will get tired of it, and that

The Collar

I shall have to go through the same crisis when the "masher" collar comes into its own again. And I shall give in. I always do.

Why cannot we leave such trivialities to women?

XX. *This Body*

THERE are occasional items of news in the papers that pull us up and tempt us to examine our attitude in regard to some question as if for the first time. One item of the kind was the announcement of the will of Edward Martyn, Irish revivalist and cousin of Mr. George Moore, in accordance with which his dead body was to be given to a medical school for dissection and the remains were afterwards to be buried, like other dissecting-room corpses, in a pauper's grave. Who, on reading this, could fail to turn round and ask himself whether he could endure the prospect of his body's being subjected, though past sense, to the knives of medical students? There are few people, indeed, who could be entirely indifferent on such a matter. If a man is careless of the fate of his body after death, as Socrates was, it is thought a sufficiently remarkable fact to be preserved in his biography. Christians ought, perhaps, of all people to have been most able to achieve this happy carelessness. But even the belief in the immortality of the soul has seldom persuaded human beings that a dead body is as worthless as the husk of a seed that has burst out of darkness into a flower. In the result, Christians have for centuries paid honour

This Body

to dead bodies as though they were more noble than the living, and many a poor man has never had the hats of passers-by raised to him till he has driven through the streets as a corpse. I do not know how far modern Christians believe that after long ages at the sound of a trumpet the body that has been the prey of worms and of dusty time will actually rise out of the earth, recomposed into the likeness of a living man. Probably there are few who would now confess to any certainty about the matter. But many good men in the past believed that the dead body, far from being a worthless garment that the soul had cast off for ever, was the very garment that the soul would resume on its exaltation into Paradise. Even those Christians who despised the body alive glorified it in death, and a saint's body that he had kept starved and unclean as beneath contempt was revered after death as something with a divine power to perform miracles. This may seem, and is, paradoxical, but the awe of the living in presence of a dead body is natural to reflecting men. Certain savages, we are told, pay honour to the bodies of the dead only because they fear that, if they do not, the spirits of the dead will haunt them. But the civilized man, who has no such terrors, is as reverent because, perhaps, he sees in the dead body a sign and wonder that changes the aspect of the world for him and brings him to the very door of the mystery of his own life.

The Peal of Bells

Whatever be the reason, the world has not yet outgrown the feeling that the dead must be honoured and not treated as refuse. The outcry during the War against the supposed German "corpse-factory," in which dead soldiers were turned into useful oils or chemicals for the munition factories, was something more than an expression of propagandist hypocrisy. It was absurd to believe that the Germans, being human beings, would sanction such a thing; but it was natural to believe that, if they did, they would themselves be so much the less human beings. And yet, if it is right to use a dead man's body for purposes of medicine, there is no logical reason why it should be a crime to use a dead man's body for purposes of war. It is arguable, indeed, that the needs of war are the more urgent, and that therefore the "corpse-factory" should be less horrifying to us than the dissecting-room. As a matter of fact, the dissecting-room would horrify us a great deal more if it were not that we have nationalized (or municipalized) the bodies of friendless paupers. When anatomists sent their scouts into the graveyards to dig up the dead who had died solvent, the friends of the dead leagued themselves together and guarded the body by night till it had rotted in the earth. How many of us in our childhood grew up amid a thousand-and-one tales of body-snatchers! What devils they and the kidnappers seemed! How thrilling to hear of their adventures! We might laugh at them, as

This Body

at the crimes of Bluebeard, but we laughed uneasily. Yet in another thousand years men may be looking back on the body-snatchers and kidnappers as among the saints of science, and Burke and Hare may be honoured as martyrs. I do not think they will, but it is possible at least that science progressed as a result of their crimes. There is certainly as much to be said in reason for allowing the dissecting-room to choose its bodies casually from the graveyards as for giving it the right to use its lancets on the unclaimed bodies of paupers. But, as most of us hope that neither we nor our friends will end even in these costly days in the workhouse, we are content with the present compromise, and we scarcely ask ourselves how the dissecting-rooms are to be supplied when poverty has been abolished. No doubt there will always be enough men and women with such a religious devotion to science that they will volunteer for the dissecting-room in their wills. But our first instinct, if volunteers were called for, would be to shrink as if from a painful sacrifice.

I, for one, should find it difficult to bequeath my body into the reckless hands of medical students. I do not know why, except that I cannot help somehow or other identifying my body with myself. Socrates was philosopher enough, on the eve of his death, to see his body as a shell and to say to himself: "That is not I." Most of us, however, though we might admit in our intelligences that our bodies were not we, would continue to think of them as ourselves in our imaginations. Whatever our essence, it is through the body that we have visited the earth, and we cannot dissociate from it any of the experiences that have made life so well worth living that we wish to go on with it. Our body was at least our inseparable consort, whether we went to church or to the tavern, whether we found our happiness in the sunny waist of the earth or by a coal fire at home, whether we played in the nursery or were kings of the football field, or fell in love or were rewarded with the great public prizes of the world. There has not been a single experience of our lives that would have been possible without hands, feet, heart, lungs, brain, mouth, eyes and ears. It is no wonder that St. Francis, on his death-bed, apologized to his body for having used it so ill, for without it there would have been no St. Francis, and the birds would have gone without their only sermon. How, then, can we be indifferent to such an associate? If a church made from the stones of the hills becomes sacred through associations, so that men, on entering it, take off their hats out of reverence for the temple of God, how much less surprising is it that a man should take thought for the fate of his body that is made of flesh and bones! Many men even leave instructions that honours shall be paid to their dead bodies such as they never demanded during life, like the Ulster Unionist who asked that his body should

This Body

be wrapped in a Union Jack and taken out and buried in Britannia's sea. Others have died the more easily because they knew that their remains (as the phrase goes) would be buried in some particular place—on the top of a hill, or in a cemetery with ghostly headstones visible from the sea at evening, or under the trees by an old church in a half-deserted village. I myself should feel melancholy if I thought I was to be buried in the Sahara or even in one of the colonies, and for a long time I should have felt a sharp pang if it had been foretold that I should be buried anywhere except in my own country, and I was particular even as to the exact spot in that. I do not know if I care so much as I once did. I fancy I have a growing objection to being buried anywhere at all. Nor do I take to the prospect of being burned. So long as one thinks of one's body as a living thing, one can hardly imagine an end to it that does not seem almost as horrible as the dissecting-table. To be perpetuated as a mummy—who would care for that? Better to be cleansed swiftly by the earth into a skeleton in a Christian grave. When I had just left school and thought I was a pantheist, I used to take a sentimental pleasure, as other boys have done, in the prospect that flowers would spring from my tomb. I even liked the thought that I should help to fertilize the earth for those flowers. I cannot comfort myself so easily now, though I should be the happier if I thought the gardener would occasionally pay some small attention to my coverture. But I have really no taste for the underworld, and, if it were possible, I do not think I should ever visit it, but should continue on the floor of this excellent earth as long as the Wandering Jew. It is said that in the end men grow tired of the body, and are glad enough to leave it. Those who do, I fancy, are bolder spirits than I. I am naturally a stay-at-home, and the only home in which I have lived all my life is my body. Born under Saturn, I have nevertheless been happy enough never to wish to change it for a better. If I have wished to be a better man, I have still wished for the new spirit to inhabit the same body, for, though it is a body that no man could be proud of, not being built in any of the noble styles of architecture, I am used to it and am bound to it by all manner of sympathies. Not that I have looked after it as well as I might have done. I have allowed it to sink into dilapidation and disrepair, so that it already resembles more than it should a piece of antiquity. But even the crooked man with the crooked cat probably lived happily enough in his crooked little house, and would not have left it without compulsion. Hence, though I cannot share their faith, I should not be sorry to think that those Christians were right who believe that on the last day the body will be whisked through the air to become the house of the soul again in a better world. I do not defend myself or pretend that

This Body

this is a laudable attitude. I admire Socrates, indeed, and all those who have despised the body as a fragile pot or as grass that withers, but I cannot help recognizing the fact that I am not of their company.

On the other hand, I cannot go so far as those people who shrink from the grave all the more because they cannot endure the thought of the rain beating down upon them by night and chilling their senseless bones. I read somewhere lately that, when the woman he loved died, Abraham Lincoln was almost driven mad during a storm by the feeling that the wind was howling and the rain falling on her grave. Others have told me that they share this feeling, and I know a man who said that he would hate to be buried in a certain graveyard because it was "very damp." But then he was subject to rheumatism. His objection was as valid, however, as is the objection of most of us to lie, misshapen and skinny, under the eyes of a professor on the dissecting-table. We impute to our dead bodies many of the senses and shames of the living, and we shudder without reason at the thought of things occurring to them that could injure us only while we are alive. Thus do we give ourselves an extension of life in our fancies. It seems as though we must be surer that life is worth living than that death is worth dying. But, even on this matter, there is room for hope.

XXI. *Change*

IT is astonishing what a difference a still morning of sunshine can make to the face of London. On such a morning, London ceases to be merely a shabby collection of shops and lodgings and becomes a charming city of pleasure as open to the sun as a country lane. The shining bodies of the motor-cars swarming in the streets begin to seem as natural in the air as insects, and, indeed, the few that have been painted in bright colours—scarlet or blue or green or yellow—amuse the eye like the first butterflies of the season. I hope the artists who have lately been conspiring to transform railway stations will afterwards turn their attention to motor-cars, and will help to bring about a time when motor-cars in the streets of a city will be as gaudy and attractive toys as the blue-and-red country carts that bump along the roads in one's memories of childhood. It may have been only a coincidence that I saw several of these coloured cars on the first certain day of spring. But they seemed like flying messengers of the change that was everywhere transmuting town from a builder's yard into a habitation on the bank of a great stream. The first sun of spring seems actually to create a new earth before our eyes. The plane-

Change

trees, which are essentially the trees of the streets, now seem exquisitely beautiful with thousands of little dark balls hanging in their bare and delicate branches. The leafless oaks in the park rise from the earth like flames of fire fed from underground. There are few flowers as yet and few songs, but at least we have that delighted knowledge that we are in the theatre and that the play is going to begin. Or, perhaps, it has already begun. The Serpentine has become a shining lake of boats, and, as they move this way and that, the sunlight reflected from the water is shimmering on their newly varnished sides. The drakes paddling their way through the water, as the sun falls on them, are rivals of peacocks and kingfishers in their heads and necks. How contentedly they wag their curly tails from side to side! How sleepily they turn up the whites of their eyes as they cruise along the edge of the water, dreaming of manna that will fall from the hands of children and nurse-maids! A duck even opens her bill in a luxurious and ludicrous yawn. Tufted ducks, little and long-haired piebalds with eyes bright as daffodils, dart hither and thither among the rain of food, more greedy than brave, and dive trickily under the water, leaving a trail of bubbles and emerging later as suddenly as jack-in-the-boxes. Sparrows almost sing as they hop about among the crumbs and bathe themselves with enthusiasm in the crisped and shallow waters as only city-dwellers bathe. Sea-gulls, the brown patch spreading over their heads, are diving down the air like rooks before a storm, and seem to be engaged in a dance in which there is a continual change of partners. The whiteness of their bodies, as the sun flashes on them, transforms London into a harbour town, just as the blue-tit's feathers, as he hangs head downwards with the light glancing on him, transform London into a Persian garden. London, it may be, looks for the most part to-day as it looked yesterday, but the sun, merely by emphasizing the colour of a bird's feather or by lighting up a blue field of sky beyond the black and bare tree-branches, or by showing the reflection of a dipping oar in the water, deceives us into imagining that a new world has been created, and we accept the tiniest detail of brightness as though it were the full payment of spring.

It is probable, indeed, that none of us sees more than a few details in the world about us at any time, and, if the world is re-created for us, it is always by some small and to others scarcely noticeable thing—a woman's face, a harbour of fishing-boats, a thrush's song, a pair of white bullocks ploughing under the olive-trees. Any of these things may be clues to that happier world into which the imagination is always trying to escape. Or it may be that they prove to us that the happier world is already about us and that we had only to open our eyes in order to see it. It is certainly strange that men and women should be so easily trans-

Change

ported from one existence into another by some newly seen thing that may not even interest their neighbours. We spend our days in a quest and become different beings when we have found the object of it, like a child that has discovered a bee-orchis for the first time. Of all quests the quest of the observer of living creatures, I think, is one of the most pleasant. His is an amusement that is continually changing the face of the world for him. He may see very little happening, but he lives in the constant expectation that something is going to happen, so that even in adverse circumstances he retains something of the unreasonable cheerfulness of Mr. Micawber. His pursuit would seem to many people extremely unsatisfying. He will spend hours looking through field-glasses and see nothing for his pains. On Sunday I saw two of his sanguine band standing outside the railings of a wood in Richmond Park and staring through their field-glasses into a thick tangle of trees. Occasionally, from the depth of the wood, you could hear ugly croaking sounds as of geese mimicking the bark of a dog. Nothing was visible, however, but the black masses of huge nests in distant tree-tops, and towards these the field-glasses were directed. "I think there's a bird in that one to the left," said a young man, pointing to a nest; "I see something white." And, indeed, even with the naked eye you could see something white, which, if you did not know it must be a heron, might have been a handkerchief or a piece of old newspaper caught in the branches. To each of us, however—for I, too, am a prey to this sort of curiosity—every bark gave pleasure, and, when the young man cried, "I think I saw it move," we envied him so fortunate an experience. A child took the glasses, and after a long look said, "I think I see the stripey feathers on its throat," and each of us in turn tried to see the stripey feathers on its throat, so that we might be level with her. But there was such a jungle of concealing branches between us and the nest that the heron was the merest blur and, except to the imagination, was as uninteresting as a daub of grey paint. Yet to each of us, I suppose, the world then seemed to be populated with herons, and we should have contradicted vehemently anyone who suggested that we were wasting our time in watching a heron that could not in fact be seen. We even discussed the question whether the spot of white was taking part in the clamour of the tree-tops, some holding that it was, and the child opposing. We strained our eyes, hoping to see its beak open, and, when the bird moved again, it seemed a notable event. Alas! it was like trying to read an undecipherable manuscript. If we had wished to study the ways of the heron, we should have done far better to go back to Captain Knight's film of the tree-tops at the Polytechnic than to stand here outside the iron bars in the foolish hope that the herons would come out and perform for us. I doubt, however, if it was the habits of herons that primarily interested us. It was not learning that we were in pursuit of. We were in quest of some experience of the eye that would suddenly reveal to us what a delightful, unfamiliar and winged world we lived in. The cinema is all very well as a record of other people's experiences, but we are ultimately dissatisfied with other people's experiences and demand experiences of our own. A bird in the bush is worth an aviary on the pictures. A bird on the pictures, indeed, is only a lesson; but a bird that we see ourselves awakens a sleeping world to life. When a heron did at last rise on its cloudy wings and disappear over the wood, the young man, I am sure, was infinitely more excited than if he had seen the whole daily life of the bird, as it fished and returned home to disgorge its catch for its gluttonous nestlings, set forth in a series of animated photographs. It was not that he had never seen a heron flying before. But there are certain things that, however often repeated, remove the film of custom from our eyes and enable us to see the world as the excellent Noah's Ark that it is, and the flight of a heron is one of them.

I passed on from the wood and went down the slope towards Pen Ponds, where I found another man—an elderly gentleman with white hair—standing on the marshy edge of the water with field-glasses inquisitive. The larger pond, indeed, is a haunt of elderly gentlemen with field-glasses, for

The Peal of Bells

here the Londoner can see fairly close at hand that strange fowl, the great crested grebe. It is a bird famous for the comedy of its courtship, and this is the season of the year—or the end of the season—at which it performs its flirtation-dance most noisily and with ruffs spread gloriously. There is no more ridiculous caress in the world than when the two birds confront each other in the water, and seem to rise breast to breast and swing their heads from side to side, and tilt at each other with their bills. Then they duck and fling back their heads acrobatically as if trying to touch the base of their necks with them, and, after a shake of their ruffled crowns, they suddenly subside into peace-loving mates floating with their lime-white breasts over the surface of the water. One sparring-match of this kind succeeded another on Sunday morning, occasionally to be interrupted by an intrusive male who dashed into the water angrily between a happy pair and broke up their clamorous argument. Sometimes you would see a solitary male swimming swiftly with neck stretched out level with the water and honking like a mechanical toy, till meeting a lonely female he would raise his crest, and the two long dark necks would rise above the white breasts and, bill to jabbing bill, the birds would circle round each other in the water as in a dance. There are certainly few odder spectacles to be seen near London than the courtship of the grebes. It is surprising, in the circumstances, that so few old gentle-

Change

men go out with their field-glasses to see them. If crested grebes were as numerous as ducks, I fancy I should tire of them sooner than of ducks, for there is something foreign in their antics, and the grebe has no music to equal the loud quack of a duck, which is surely one of the most beautiful sounds in nature. I never hear a duck quacking across the Serpentine towards evening but a whole landscape rises before me, blotting out London and substituting a country pond, and fields, and hedges running down into meadows, and beyond the meadows a river running into the sea, and the sun setting just out of reach of a long and shadowy headland. It transforms a city into a happy solitude, and so enables me to travel without leaving home. London is, perhaps, most delightful of all as the scene of such transformation-scenes as this. If I were living far away in the country among real farmyard ducks, it is possible that I might be enjoying transformation-scenes that blotted out the fields and the hedges and showed me London.

XXII. *Worry*

THE bookmaker was a huge black-browed, red-faced man with a paunch that, when once he had sat down in a chair, kept him sitting there for the rest of the evening. He sat in the smoking-room of the hotel, looking as gloomy as the king who never smiled again. Other bookmakers sat round the fire in other chairs, and occasionally, though not often, one of them made, or attempted to make, a joke. But the huge black-browed man showed scarcely any sign of interest, and, if the joker turned round to him as though expecting a laugh, he merely said in a deep funereal voice: "Wot are you going to 'ave, Bob?" He joined in the conversation, indeed, only to order drinks or to endorse some pessimistic remark that had been made. He mourned with the others over the death of a fellow bookie—a good fellow who hadn't been worth a quid one day, was worth twenty thousand six months later, spent it like a man and died. "He was a good fellow, was Bill," said one, "and good fellows never last." "No, good fellows never last," the others agreed, while Christians and Jews took a sip of something and sighed as they thought of their own fates. The huge man

Worry

turned his head on his neck with difficulty and stared at the company with eyes that looked like two open graves. "Did you ever know a good man to last?" he challenged them; "did anybody 'ere ever know a good man to last?" They nodded approval, for their thoughts were morbid owing to the large sums of money they had had to pay out to the public over the victory of Sir Galahad III in the Lincolnshire Handicap, and their hearts were full of fear lest they should have to pay out a still larger sum of money if Conjuror II should on the following day win the Grand National. "They say that a quarter of a million 'as gone to France over the Lincoln," said a young Jew in the corner. "It 'asn't gone yet," said the black-browed man. "'Ow d' you mean ' 'asn't gone yet'?" asked the other. "Wot I mean is," was the reply, "the French 'as won a quarter of a million, but will they git it?" "W'y wouldn't they git it?" "W'y wouldn't they git it?" repeated the black-browed man impatiently, "w'y *would* they git it, if the money isn't there to pay?" "They'll never see some of it," a man with a sandy beard agreed. "If a bookmaker can't pay, 'e can't pay. That seems plain enough," said the big man; "it ain't 'is fault; it ain't anybody's fault. 'E's beat and 'e knows it. It might 'appen to the best man in the world." "Everybody gets knocked some time," observed the sandy man. "Everybody as was ever born," the big man supported him. "It don't say w'ether 'e's a good man or a bad man.

The Peal of Bells

'E can't pay, and 'e gets knocked. It might 'appen to the best man as was ever born."

A draper in a morning coat, with thinning hair above his temples and with dapper spats on his feet, who looked like an inebriated cockatoo about to deliver an address at a Pleasant Sunday Afternoon, leaned forward in his wooden arm-chair and, gesticulating with his pipe, said: "And the same thing would happen, my dear friend, in every business house in England, if it were suddenly called on to pay all its debts. Take the Post Office even. Do you think that if all the people who have deposited fifty million pounds in the Post Office Savings Bank were to call round to-morrow morning and ask for their money, the Post Office could pay them? The fifty million pounds simply aren't there. How is all the business of the country run? Credit. Isn't that right? Correct me if I am wrong. Is there any other business in England that is expected to pay its debts at such short notice as a bookmaker's? Tell me if I am wrong, my friend. Isn't the whole basis of the stability of English prosperity simply credit?" The big man looked a little puzzled by the long speech of the draper, but he nodded gloomily and said: "That's so. Credit," and then, changing the subject: "Wot are you going to 'ave, Bob?" Bob said that he was seventy years old and gouty and wasn't able to drink so much as he used to, but that he would have just one more—a little drop of "the cratur." "Ah," he said, his eyes shining with a glow of reminiscent affection, "it's donkey's years ago since I used to go over to Ireland twice or three times a year, but I never sit up at night having a drop of 'the cratur' like this without thinking about them. You know, boys, I love the Irish. Good fellows—good fellows to a man. Somebody said good fellows never last. Well, that's true enough. Tom Rooney's dead, and Barney Rudge, and Jack the Scotchman who came from Belfast. And I could name dozens more. All good fellows. And all dead." He drained his glass at a gulp. The big man did the same, and, as the waiter appeared, somebody else said: "Another before you go, Bob." Bob declared again that he was seventy years old and had the gout and that he had to get up in the morning, but that he would just have one more for the sake of the boys. "An Irishman," he went on, when the waiter had taken the orders, "will always help another Irishman. He's like a Jew that way. That's what I like about them. If there's a bit of business he can't do, he'll pass it on to another Irishman. An Englishman won't do that. Here it's every man for himself." The big man nodded behind a long cigar. "That's right," he said; "an Englishman always crabs another Englishman." It amused me to find Dr. Johnson's judgment on the national characteristics of the two peoples reversed a century and a half later in a company of bookmakers. I put it down, however, largely to the victory of Sir

The Peal of Bells

Galahad at Lincoln, which had undoubtedly done a great deal to convince Englishmen in the bookmaking business that their country was on its last legs. "It isn't like wot it used to be," they told each other sadly. "Nobody seems to 'ave any money. And, if they 'ave, they won't spend it. Gorblimey, this isn't the England you and I knew, Bob, thirty years ago." "Wot's going to win to-morrow?" asked the young Jew. "Ask me another," said the big man; "all I know is that, if Conjuror II wins to-morrow, some of us may as well go into the workhouse." " 'Ave another drink first," said the Jew flippantly, and called to the waiter: "Drinks all round, Sam!" The man with the sandy beard repeated for the nth time that he was seventy years old, that he wasn't able to drink so much as he once was, that the Jew could never have had the gout or he would know that the only thing to do was to go slow, but that, however, another drink wouldn't hurt him, perhaps, but that after that he must go to bed—positively. I will say this to his credit that at last he kept his word, and after him yawning bookmaker after yawning bookmaker rose from his chair, stretched himself, said "Good night all!" and disappeared from the room.

At last there was nobody left in the room but the cockatoo draper, the big man and myself. "My friend," said the draper, as the big man also began to yawn and to rub the sleep from his eyes, "you don't look particularly cheerful." "No," agreed

Worry

the big man, "and I don't feel it. Wot's there to be cheerful about? Seems to me this country's got into a blooming mess. Nobody's got any money, and everybody 'oo 'as is out on strike." "Granted, my friend," said the draper, wagging an argumentative finger; "I grant you all that. But, at the same time, dark though the clouds are, I think I see the sunshine breaking through." "Strikes, strikes everywhere," the big man went on, ignoring the rhetoric. "Wot I mean is, w'ere is it going to end?" "Now wait a moment," the draper checked him; "wait a moment and let us study the present in the light of history." " 'Istory," said the other, "wot's 'istory got to do with it?" "One moment, my friend," the draper appealed to him with a persuasive smile; "probably I have read more than you have." "P'raps you 'ave," agreed the big man, though in a tone that suggested that, perhaps, on the other hand, he had not. "Have you ever, for instance," the draper pressed him, "studied the history of the fall of the Roman Empire?" "Can't say I 'ave," admitted the bookmaker. "Well, then," said the draper triumphantly, "I was reading a book about it only last week, a book by a very great scholar indeed, and he made it perfectly clear that the Roman Empire fell for two reasons. Now, what do you think those two reasons were?" "Aven't an ideer," said the bookmaker, looking as if he would have given a great deal not to be so fat that it was difficult to go to bed. "The two reasons why the Roman Empire fell, according to this great scholar," the draper told him, pointing the mouthpiece of his pipe at him impressively, "were corruption and inflation. Well now." "Well now, wot?" "Well now, just listen to me a moment. Compare those days to ours. What are we suffering most from to-day?" "Strikes." "Ah, my friend, but what causes the strikes?" "Gord knows. Look at these blooming bus-drivers. Wot are *they* striking for?" "Keep to the point, my friend, keep to the point. The causes that are producing all these strikes to-day are exactly the same causes that brought about the downfall of the Roman Empire a thousand—well, a very long time before either you or I were born." "Don't let's trouble about before me and you was born." "I was trying to tell you, if you would only have a little patience, my friend, that the causes of the strikes, not before we were born, but at the present day——" "I thought you said before we was born." "That the strikes that are happening at the present day under our very eyes are produced by the same two causes that brought about the downfall of the Roman Empire——" "I thought you said you wasn't talking about the Roman Empire." "Corruption and inflation," almost shouted the draper, thumping the arm of his chair irascibly; "corruption and inflation." "Let's 'ave another drink," said the bookmaker, as the night boots put his head in at the door to see what the noise was about. "Thank

Worry

you," said the draper, recovering himself. "A small Scotch whisky and a baby Polly; and, if you can follow my argument, it is this—that we have now got in this country the best Government England ever had, and that it's going to put a stop to these things. I'm a Conservative myself, but I believe that Mr. Ramsay MacDonald is an honest man and that he intends to tackle these two great problems, corruption and inflation." "Well," said the bookmaker, paying for the drinks; "I don't know much about politics. I'm in favour of Conservative or Labour or anybody else that gives a man a chance." "Exactly what Mr. Ramsay MacDonald means to do, my friend." "That's wot I say. Give a man a chance. I mean, w'y can't there be a kind of a way of kind of coming to some kind of an agreement so as to stop these blooming strikes. I mean to say, wot's the sense of it all? I mean, wot are these bloomin' bus-men striking about?" "I've just told you, my friend. Fundamentally, corruption and inflation." "Seems to me this country's 'eading for a revolution. Looks as if we're in a blooming 'ole. I meant to say, wot's going to 'appen?" "The revolution's going to happen, my friend, unless Mr. Ramsay MacDonald can put a stop to corruption and inflation." "But can 'e? 'Ow can 'e? Can 'e stop the blooming bus-strike? I tell you straight I don't like the look of things. I'm beginning," he declared, as he helped himself out of his chair, and, having achieved

The Peal of Bells

this, yawned like a hippopotamus, "I'm beginning to feel worried." "And so are we all, my dear friend," the draper assured him; "everybody's beginning to feel worried." "Yes," said the bookmaker, balancing his bulk before the dying fire and with the air of a man imparting a secret not meant for everybody, "and I'll tell you 'oo's worried. King George is worried. You wouldn't 'ave caught 'is father going to a football match." "That is so," agreed the draper. "Did you ever 'ear of King Edward going to a football match?" the bookmaker asked with a look of extraordinary and gloomy cunning. "Never," said the draper. "Nor anybody else," said the bookmaker, and walked carefully, lugubriously and triumphantly to the door.

XXIII. *In the Casino*

EACH day, as I left the hotel for the Casino, I had to pass a house which bore the name, "Jacasse." I could not help looking at it, and, every time I looked at it, the word "Jacasse" looked back at me in large letters from the glass window above the door. It was almost as though the house spoke, like a parrot or a raven. "Going to win it all back to-night," I might be day-dreaming at the back of my mind as I advanced up the road; but, as sure as I began to believe it, I would look up and catch sight of that detestable villa, which would pursue me with taunts of "Jacasse" till I was safe inside the Casino and sitting at an enticing green table with all the numbers painted on it under the chandeliers.

In theory I am opposed to gambling of this kind. To back a horse is to take part in a contest between one living creature and another—to obtain excitement from a thing that is in itself exciting even though no one is going to make a penny out of it. Is there anyone, however, who could be content to spend an evening following the fortunes of the 3 or the 5 or the 7 in the *Boule* room if no one were gambling on the event? Pythagoras, who believed that all things are numbers, might, if he were alive, play *Boule* for fun. He might enjoy the spectacle of the little red ball zigzagging its way round among the red, blue and yellow cups that contain the numbers, and might really care, without self-interest, whether, after that final hesitating wobble, it settled into a cup marked 8 or into a cup marked 9. Even a mathematician, who made a special study of chance, might find excitement in observing during the course of an evening the unequal fates of numbers each of which seems to have as good a reason for winning as its neighbour. I am neither Pythagoras nor a mathematician, however, and, though I have a favourite number, I do not like it as I like a favourite author or animal. If my number wins, I do not take any pleasure in its victory, unless I have backed it. I do not regard it as a rival of all the other numbers to the point of being able to share in its triumphs. Numbers, indeed, do not engage the heart any more than do the "heads" and "tails" of a coin. Begin to bet on numbers, however, and with how intense a fascination you can follow their ups and downs! Each of the green tables, with its croupier and his rake presiding, is surrounded by men and women, some of them sitting, more of them standing behind the chairs, all of them strung up to the necessity of making a quick choice of the numbered square on which to fling their stakes, while the man with the red ball cries "Faites vos jeux, messieurs," or "Marquez vos jeux." There is still time to gamble, while the ball rocks up and

In the Casino

down that circular honeycomb of numbers to the cry, "Les jeux sont faits." But you must make haste now, for it is beginning to circulate more slowly, and, if you do not decide at once, the fatal "Rien n'va plus" will have gone forth, and you will have to remain a spectator till the chairman proclaims the winning number, "Le neuf." But you will not have to wait long for a chance to play, for in thirty seconds the croupiers will have raked back the money from all but the winning square, will have paid out seven to one to those who were lucky enough to back it, and "égalité" to those who had backed either the odd numbers or the numbers on the right-hand band, and the cry "Marquez vos jeux" will once more be ringing down the room and the red ball be swaying round the table on its fortuitous journey. Many onlookers, I believe, find the game of *Boule* monotonous and dull. They look round the faces of the gamblers and think them nervous and joyless. It is possible that human beings who are excited about money seldom look happy. But then it is questionable if human beings look happy when they are reading detective stories or watching a sensational drama at the moving pictures. There is little occasion for laughter at the gaming tables. Game follows game too quickly to allow much leisure for comedy. There are people who stroll round the tables and throw an occasional franc on a number for amusement, and to whom it is a jest whether they win or lose.

The Peal of Bells

But, if you sit down at a table and never let the ball circulate without an attempt to foretell the number of the cup in which it will ultimately settle, you will find yourself much too deeply absorbed in a thrilling serial story of loss and gain to be able to pay attention to anything but the nine numbers and the maddening indecisions of the little red ball.

It is not that the money involved matters to you. Here, in this Casino, you need not stake more than a franc at a time, and not many of the gamblers are playing with higher than five-franc tokens. There was never a gaming-room in which it was easier to play within one's means, and anyone who wishes to risk ruin must pass through the guarded glass door into the baccarat-room. *Boule,* as played here, indeed, is an amusement for sober people of moderate means. It is an evening-dress crowd that is present, yet most of the people composing it would think they were losing heavily if they lost £5 in a week. None the less, they seem to find the game extraordinarily engrossing. They would find it engrossing, I believe, even if it were played for halfpennies. Obviously there are thrills that a man can have only by risking more than a wise man would care to risk. Most of us, however, enjoy the quick coming and going of money, even though it will make little difference one way or the other to our week's income. Philosophers may wonder that, the money itself mattering so little, we do not play for matches or for counters that can be put back into

In the Casino

a box at the end of the game. Money, however, has an imaginative lure that counters never possess, and to win even a small sum at play affords the gambler a pleasure that cannot be estimated in terms of the amount he has won. A lawyer confessed the other day that it gave him more pleasure to win £5 on a horse-race than to make £500 at the Bar. I do not think the average man would go so far as this, but even the man of moderate passions is made absurdly happy by a small windfall from the tree of fortune. To back the right number time and again at *Boule,* as I did on my first visit to the Casino, gives one a curious and irrational confidence in one's destiny. One feels exhilarated as though one had mastered a new element. Fortune is the most charming of flatterers. She tempts us almost to believe that it is through our cleverness rather than our luck that we have won. Betting and gambling would lose half their attractiveness, did they not deceive us with the fancy that there may be an element of personal merit in our winnings. Our reason may protest, but our self-love is credulous. And just as the gambler who wins a great deal feels clever, so does the gambler who loses a great deal in the course of an evening feel a fool. I, for one, if I lose twenty times running—as, indeed, I often do—though the loss of money is so small that it is hardly worth considering, am aware of a curious dip of personal humiliation, as though I had bungled my chances. I blame

The Peal of Bells

myself for having time after time put my money on the 3 when the 3 was obviously out of luck; I feel that a wise man should have foreseen that it was now time for the 5 to win again. Coming into the hall, I had met a guest from the same hotel and asked him: "What numbers are winning to-night?" He had replied: "There's a great run on the 2 and the 7." It was perfectly true. But, as often as I put my money on the 2 or the 7 it was sure to lose, and when, thinking the luck had changed, I would choose another number, it was only to see the 2 or the 7 turning up again till I went back to it. Here and there at the tables you would see a young man or an old woman jotting down in a notebook every number that won, in an attempt to discover the lucky number of the hour or to work out some infallible system. I myself have many superstitions, but not the superstition of the system. I change my table from time to time, believing that I shall have better luck at table number nine than at table number four. I sit as a rule at the left-hand side of the table, where the numbers along the band, 1, 3, 6, 8, add up to a number that I like, 18. I won lavishly on the first night by keeping almost exclusively to these numbers, and my pockets were heavy with five-franc tokens when, after midnight, I went up to the desk to change them into money. But after that, the band betrayed me. No matter where I sat, or what number I chose, it was but seldom that my

In the Casino

stake returned to me eightfold, and not many minutes after the *changeur* had given me a handful of tokens for a paper note I would have to return to him to purchase others. Not that I lost much, for I did not play high, but after the first night I lost consistently.

Luckily there are consolations for losing. "After all," I tell myself, as I go home under the moon with my pockets empty, "I'd rather my luck would come some other way than in gambling." By steadily thinking this for a few seconds, I induce a feeling of positive relief that I have lost. There must be other human beings built in the same fashion, for all nations seem to have proverbs invented for the consolation of unlucky gamblers. The human being likes to feel that he has done the best thing; and so, if he is lucky, he congratulates himself on his skill, and, if he is unlucky, he congratulates himself on having escaped a kind of luck that would bring him ill-luck in matters of greater importance. And he has yet another consolation. He tells himself that he has only to go to the Casino on the next night to "win it all back again." He does not entirely believe this, but he is exceedingly optimistic about it. Nearly everybody in the hotel is an optimist of this description. In the dining-room, table converses with table about the losses of the previous night, and no one is withdrawing from the game on that account. The good-natured grey-haired man, whose table is nearest mine, looks

The Peal of Bells

across during luncheon and makes a movement with his hand as if he were flinging coins on to a baize table. "To-night?" he asks, raising an eyebrow, and chuckles. I nod. "Going to get it all back again," I tell him. He chuckles again delightedly, as though we had exchanged the best joke in the world. Every night I meet him in the *Boule* room. He does not gamble much himself, but wanders round the tables, following the fortunes of the various gamblers from the hotel, and occasionally putting a piece on one of the squares. "I don't care much for gambling," he confides to me; "it's my wife who likes it." He looks over towards her, where she sits at one of the tables, with intense admiration. "Wonderful loser," he tells me. "Never turns a hair." Has wife ever been praised more nobly?

But all this can scarcely be called gambling. In order to see the spectacle of men and women gambling one has to go into the *Salles de Baccarat*. To do this one must show one's passport and fill a form and pay forty francs for a weekly ticket. When one enters the strictly guarded door, one realizes how innocent is the game of *Boule* that one has left behind. It is as though a different race of men and women were playing in the *Baccarat* room. They are people who eat more, and drink more, and dress more, and have more, and spend more, and play more. They include every type of the rich and reckless, from the red-faced eighteenth-

In the Casino

century old English gentleman to the cosmopolitan lady of our own time with hair and eyelids and cheeks and lips all dyed or painted different but equally unnatural colours. Pearls, diamonds and sapphires are as abundant as peas and beans in a kitchen garden. The people (who are playing *chemin de fer*) laugh a good deal more than in the *Boule* room, but they are also more flushed with excitement. And, indeed, as they sit round the little oval tables while the shoe of cards circulates, and at the end of each draw the croupier scoops up the money on his enormous paper-knife, and re-apportions it, and begins again, in the endless quest for the beautiful and victorious nine, even an onlooker can share some of the eagerness of the players. Here there is a sense of careless profusion of money, each of the gamblers with his little heap of notes and hundred-franc and twenty-franc pieces before him on the table. Here a rich or a reckless man puts up a huge bank and, all round the green oval, money-tokens will be flung down to challenge him, and, in a few minutes, so great are his gains that the croupier has to pour them into a lacquered bowl, which the winner bears off in triumph to the desk and exchanges for notes. This is the luxury of gambling, indeed, and, coming into it from the *Boule* room, I felt extraordinarily virtuous as I surveyed it. It was as though I had been a spectator at an old Drury Lane melodrama or had come on a set of characters of Mr. William Le Queux amid their glittering pleasures. If I had had enough money, I should have sat down among them, and pursued the nine for gain. As it was, I said to myself: "What lives the rich lead!" and went back to the *Boule* room, where the little red ball rolled among the numbered cups like a child's toy. How charming it seemed! How pastoral! And how economical!

XXIV. *The Quarrel*

IT is a curious fact that many people who had lost interest in Tutankhamen began to take an interest in him again as a result of Mr. Carter's quarrel with the Egyptian Government. He came to life as a mummy last year, but the active life of a mummy is briefer even than that of a human being, and he had already faded, he and his throne and his chariots and his desiccated flowers, from the imaginations of all but a few experts when Mr. Carter's quarrel came opportunely to make the dead king, the mighty one, once more real to us. The lord of life couched amid the luxuries of death—how near to us he seems in consequence of a number of ladies having been refused admission to his tomb! Dust was descending on the dust of his last home, and dullness was claiming the dead king for its own, when an angry word from Mr. Carter sent the dust and the dullness flying, and the civilized world began to feel that a quarrel about Tutankhamen was its quarrel and to take sides in a dispute over his withered skin. There is nothing like a quarrel for attracting our attention. The ordinary man does not realize the importance of anything, indeed, till somebody has begun to quarrel about it. Who knows whether

The Peal of Bells

Helen of Troy was the most beautiful woman who ever lived? Yet we find it difficult not to think so merely because she was the occasion of the most beautiful quarrel in legend or history. It is possible that more beautiful women have lived than any that ever got into the histories, but men did not lose their tempers and their lives over them; they were happily married, and their names have perished. If king strove with king's son for the possession of the plainest woman on earth, she would haunt history as a lovely ghost, and schoolboys would lose their hearts to her till the end of time. Quarrels, it seems, are more memorable than beauty. It is even, perhaps, quarrels that make beauty. Most of us are not original enough to invent our own quarrels, or we find our own quarrels petty and unsatisfying, and so we are constantly looking out for some nobler quarrel in which to take a side. We are in this matter merely degenerate knights-errant, for the knight-errant was a man who would wander through the known world in search of a good cause for a quarrel. To him a day seemed ill-spent in which he had not quarrelled with some poor scoundrel who only wished to enjoy himself. And, ever since, we have idealized the knight-errant to such a point that we have made a saint even of Don Quixote, who would quarrel with a windmill for lack of a worthier enemy. It looks as though nature had intended us to quarrel. Otherwise she would not have implanted in our

The Quarrel

breasts such a passionate interest in the contentions of our fellow-creatures. Literature is for the most part an idealization of quarrels. Cut quarrels out of literature, and you will have very little history or drama or fiction or epic poetry left. Let us cease to be quarrelsome in our tastes, and D'Artagnan will no longer stir our pulses. Dumas is the prince of narrative writers, chiefly because no other writer could so dexterously lure his characters into an incessant series of quarrels. We laugh at Donnybrook Fair as though it were something characteristically and comically Irish, but Donnybrook Fair pervades European literature from the *Iliad* to *Mr. Polly*. Everywhere are fights, brawls, squabbles, contentions. As for Homer, as though his characters could not get enough of fighting on the plains of Troy, he must needs invent additional quarrels for them and set Thersites nagging and Achilles sulking in his tent in an overflow of ill-temper.

Why nature made us so prone to quarrel and to love quarrelling it is difficult to guess; and we can scarcely tell whether the universal taste is a good or an evil. Dr. Watts, in the famous poem beginning "Let dogs delight to bark and bite," warned little children against it. But even he looked on the quarrels of dogs and bears and lions as a fulfilment of the will of God. If there is as good a case to be made out for the quarrels of human beings, it must be based, I think, on some such phi-

The Peal of Bells

losophy as that which is expressed in the Irish proverb, "Contention is better than loneliness." Contention may also be better than stagnation. It is said to be healthier to breathe bad air that circulates than to breathe good air that is perfectly still. A quarrel may act as a sort of ventilating-fan and may be the only means of making the atmosphere tolerable. Not in vain, perhaps, is it written that "the falling out of faithful friends renewing is of love." It would not be safe, however, if one were writing a book on how to be happy though in love, to lay too much stress on the importance of quarrelling. Nature gives human beings the quarrels they deserve, and there is no need to go out Quixotically in search of them. Otherwise, we should have idealists who made their quarrel as regular a part of their time-table as their morning bath; and half the charm of a quarrel is that it should be irregular and unexpected. I once met two newly married people in the street, and, in the course of conversation, the wife said to me, "Oh, we've just had our morning quarrel." She said it with an air of radiant amusement. But a cloud of sulkiness passed over the husband's face as she said it. She was the more ingenuous and had clearly no sense of sin in having lost her temper and recovered it again. He, on the other hand, was manifestly of the school of Dr. Watts, and hated to have his shame published. I do not know enough about human nature to be sure which of

The Quarrel

them was right. She, I think, was wise in not letting a past quarrel weigh on her conscience. But I sympathized with him in so far as I myself am unable either to lose my temper or to see other people losing theirs without feelings of humiliation. I once wrote an angry letter to a tailor. Even after many years, it remains in my memory to accuse me of folly. I have been guilty of worse sins, but a few ill-natured sentences written to a tailor push through the crowd to humiliate me. If only the correspondence could have continued, and if the tailor and I could have exchanged brief notes of reconciliation, even that base quarrel might have become sweet in the recollection, and, as I looked back, I should now probably be fonder of him than he deserves. But the letters broke off abruptly; a sneer from me, a sneer from him, and the tailor and I were divided for ever. I wonder if he, too, has been grieving all these years. If I wrote to him to-morrow, saying that I was sorry, would he write back to me, "Sir, you are a gentleman," and dissolve two hearts in tenderness? Alas, though I know that all quarrels should end in this manner, I am too shy to write after so long an interval, and his hairs and mine will grow greyer and fewer without either of us ever knowing whether the other has forgiven him. Quarrel, then, if you must, but see to it that every quarrel ends in a reconciliation. This is true alike of quarrels with tailors and of those larger quarrels called wars. A quarrel that

The Peal of Bells

has not a happy ending (which means a quarrel that is not forgotten) is worse than a bad conscience.

Quarrels, we may conclude, may be useful as a medicine for certain diseases of human nature. The history of wars does not suggest that they are a very effective means of restoring the health of the world, but it is possible to argue that they are a desperate remedy to which the human race will always turn if it can find no better means of persuading men to endure living in the same world with each other. The unity of England is the consequence of the quarrels of several petty kingdoms —quarrels which have long since ended in a general reconciliation; and it may even be that, if the kingdoms and the republics of the earth go on quarrelling long enough, this may result in a grand reconciliation which will bring about the unity of any mankind that happens to be left. That the health of the world can be preserved by other methods seems obvious enough nowadays to thoughtful men. But, if we do not attempt those other methods, be sure that Nature will do her best to restore the health of the nations by an endless series of quarrels; and mankind will eventually learn its lesson, and live at peace. It is at least a hopeful sign that for centuries we have been constantly inventing moral equivalents of quarrelling—in the drama and in sport, for instance. We have the sham quarrels of mighty contestants in cricket and in football, and every day of the week some struggle between

The Quarrel

such teams as Wolverhampton Wanderers and Tottenham Hotspur seems to hundreds of thousands of Englishmen an affair of more thrilling import than the wars of Carthage and Rome. Here and in the arts we may be purging ourselves of the quarrelsomeness with which we were born. Those who are always on the look-out for signs of the degradation of our times are continually denouncing us for playing the part of spectators at our games, but it is conceivable that in the multiplication of spectators as compared with contestants lies one of the greatest hopes for the future of the human race. There will never be anything but tumult so long as we cannot see a quarrel without taking a practical part in it. There are some men who long to interfere even in a private quarrel; others can withhold themselves from a private but not from a public one. There is a famous Irish story that while a fight was in progress in the street, a man, looking out of an upper window, called to his daughter: "Mary, I wish you would go to the door and bring me word if this is a private or a public dispute." He could have remained a spectator of the one, but not of the other. Thus we change with the centuries, and the change is probably due in some measure to the fact that, where man was once a knight-errant, he is now a sportsman. He will still engage in quarrels, but he is convinced by now that he should engage in them only as a last resort. He is happiest, indeed, when he has hired other men to quarrel for him in a playing-field, and

The Peal of Bells

he gets as much pleasure from this make-believe strife as his ancestors ever got from shedding blood. Had Aristotle lived in a sporting age, he might have extended his theory of katharsis from the theatre to the playground. In sport we have made quarrels amusing and have eliminated most of their dangers. We are undoubtedly getting on.

XXV. *Laziness: Written in Winter*

IN the minds of most of us laziness is associated with warmth—with summer and islands in the South Seas. No doubt, it is pleasanter to be lazy in summer than in winter—on a South Sea island than at the North Pole—but, from my own experience, I should say that the antipathy to work becomes greater as the temperature falls. In theory we ought to work harder in cold climates and in cold seasons, because there is so little temptation to do anything else. Our one object is to seek refuge from Nature, and to distract our thoughts from the bleak and songless world outside. You might think that in such circumstances we would resign ourselves to toil till the sun returned, but in plain fact we do not. There is something of the hibernating animal in each of us, and our energies fall asleep with the first east wind of November. There are false dawns of revival during a spell of hoar frost, which stimulates us like a sparkling wine so that we imagine that we have not only recovered our full energies, but added to them. But in a day or two the thaw comes, and our imagined energy melts like a snow man, and we sink into a grey and woolly nothingness again and are happy only because we remember that it was once summer, and know that every day that passes is taking us twenty-four hours nearer spring. But,

The Peal of Bells

after all, the whole course of human history ought to have taught us that laziness is born not of the heat but of the cold. The first races that were energetic enough to civilize themselves lived in the south, and even to-day, with all our hot-water bottles and other aids to make-believe warmth, we of the north cannot equal the achievements of a little sunny town in Greece that made itself master of the Ægean more than two thousand years ago. We attribute the greatness of Athens and of Rome to the supreme genius of their people, but the better part of the genius of the Greeks and the Romans was merely the absence of our frigid northern stiffness. They lived under a sky under which it was possible even to work with their brains—the most difficult of all forms of work, and that which most distinguishes us from the beasts—and, as a result, they gave the world philosophies and poems which the average northerner is too lazy even to read. The reason why English men and women prefer *If Winter Comes* to Plato is that they live in too cold a climate to be able to work hard enough with their brains to follow Plato's arguments. It is a significant fact that Scotsmen, who are the most natively intellectual of the northern races, always fly south when possible on reaching the age of maturity. They do so, not (as has been vulgarly suggested) from greed, but in search of a climate worthy of their brains. The cold north, indeed, in comparison with the warm south, is idle, barren and incompetent. It has pro-

Laziness: Written in Winter

duced no Bible, no *Iliad*, no Parthenon, no Michel Angelo. Every period in which its genius has flowered has been a period in which it drew its inspiration from the south. Take Italy from the map, and you will lose Chaucer and Shakespeare as well as Dante. Take Judea from the map, and we should still all be pagans mouthing in a saga. Until a handful of Italian soldiers came to England, the Britons were too indolent even to dress themselves, and I sometimes wonder whether the story that they painted themselves with woad may not have arisen from the fact that they were fantastically blue with their native cold.

These things I pondered as I lay in my bed on a cold February morning and found myself unable to make the necessary effort to get up. The air outside the window was a grey and repulsive ocean. Little waves of it broke on my pillow and trickled down my shoulders. I shivered and drew the bedclothes closer about me, and thought desperately of the work that I had to do. The telephone bell rang —the telephone is in my bedroom, but not within reach of my bed—and I turned my head round and looked at the receiver hostilely. "It may be a wrong call," I told myself, and watched its expressionless mouth, hoping that the bell would stop ringing before I was compelled to get up and answer it. There is no use in getting angry with a telephone. Had I been a hero in fiction, I might have picked up Boswell's *Life of Johnson* from the table beside the bed

The Peal of Bells

and flung it at it. But I am temperamentally gentle to inanimate objects, and I lay back on the pillow resignedly, hoping that some one else in the house would hear the telephone and hurry in to answer it. As no one came, and as my patience became exhausted by the din of the bell, I threw back the blankets, sprang out on to the floor, and crossed the room. The receiver was like a block of Polar ice as I took it up in my hand. I felt like shouting "Halloa!" in a fierce voice, but either I had not the courage or I was too much shaken with the cold, and I spoke in weak, piping accents that can have conveyed nothing of my resentment at being disturbed in this inhuman fashion. It turned out to be a call of not the slightest importance—a message that could easily have been put on a postcard and delivered through the letter-box at an hour when the house had become more or less lukewarm. I answered with courtesy, however, a weak-kneed Bayard in pyjamas, and even expressed a hope that the nephew's measles were better. But, when I put back the receiver, I was feeling so chilled to the marrow that there was nothing for it but to creep back into bed again, and try to get warm enough to be able to begin on the day's work. There was very urgent and important work waiting for me. The previous night I had left word that I was to be called an hour earlier than usual in order to get it finished. I had been called as I requested, but it is an inexplicable fact that a knock on the door on a cold morning,

Laziness: Written in Winter

instead of waking me, has the exactly opposite effect of putting me into a profound sleep. Even those who suffer from insomnia, I am told, fall into a doze as soon as the morning tap comes on the door. I know a lady who has the theory that the only way to make sure of a good night's sleep would be to arrange to be knocked up hourly during the night from one o'clock onwards in order to get that exquisite feeling of somnolence that follows when one has called out: "Thank you, I'm getting up at once." People say that you sleep still sounder if hot water has been left outside the door or if there is a pot of tea to be allowed to grow cold on a tray at the bedside. There are men, I know, who are incapable of this subtlety of behaviour and who respond to a morning knock like a slave to a master's whip. They have turned themselves into machines as regular as their clocks, and lead the lives of well-conducted Robots. It is, perhaps, necessary that a certain proportion of the human race should live after this fashion, but I wonder whether the people who get up so regularly and so early in the morning ever ask themselves whether they do not put into the effort of getting up a great deal of energy that might well be reserved for more important tasks. Some of them are so busy being punctual that they have no time to do what you and I would call work. The idlest people I have ever known were men who rose early in the morning and went about for the rest of the day busily doing nothing. The man who is addicted to

The Peal of Bells

early rising is more likely to fuss than to work, and his day is for the most part a trivial drama of pretended activities. Let it not be thought that I wish to disparage the virtue of the man who leaves his bed betimes, not as a matter of habit, but in obedience to a lofty purpose. No one admires more than I do the matutinal enthusiasm of those gallant bathers who plunge into the Serpentine even though the snow is falling. There is something noble in self-conquest when it is carried to such a pitch as this. You may look on it as a form of self-torture comparable to the hair shirt of the monk. But I have a profound respect for the monk in his hair shirt and, though I do not envy him his hair shirt, I envy him the self-control that enables him to go on wearing it when he might be clothed like one of the statues outside Horne Brothers' shop at the corner of New Oxford Street. I think, indeed, we should all admire the early riser if we were sure that he rose from virtue and not from habit. I myself have aspired after virtue of this kind ever since my schooldays. How often, at night, have I taken an alarum-clock up to the bedroom and diligently set it for seven—nay, for six—and seen myself in my mind's eye, a pale Faustus, turning over the pages of the classics with frozen fingers before the sun was up! Of all the moral luxuries known to man, there is none to surpass that which can be got from winding an alarum-clock and setting it for an hour when not even a housemaid or a milkman will be stirring. Alarum-

Laziness: Written in Winter

clocks, however, delightful though they are as moral stimulants, have one fault: they go off. There is nothing more disturbing than the damnable iteration of that tinny bell breaking the silence of a cold winter's morning. There was no mechanical means of stopping the clock in our house, and again and again I have had to rise from bed and thrust the soap between the clapper and the metal in order to be able to finish my night's sleep. It is surely a proof of the persistency of idealism in the human breast that, even after this had happened a score of times, I still continued to wind the alarum every night, hesitating only as to whether I should set it for six or for seven, and usually ending with a compromise at the intervenient half-hour. How happy one feels when one has at last decided when to be wakened! With how good a conscience one goes to sleep! I am positive that when I lay sleeping, after such an experience of spiritual self-conquest, I must have looked as calm and as innocent as a child in an angel-guarded bed.

Even to-day, though I have long since given up alarum-clocks as an incitant to virtue, I find myself at least once a week leaving word that I should like to be called at some heroically early hour the next morning. I do not, it is true, get up in the morning when I am called, but I like to stake out these anticipatory claims to the higher life, and, though it irritates servants, I cannot help feeling that it does me good and keeps the lamp of perfection burning with however tiny a flame. Sometimes I tell myself

The Peal of Bells

that it is mere weakness of will to resolve upon a thing at night and not to perform it in the morning. But, to be quite honest, the world in which one goes to bed is not the same place as the world into which one wakes up. At midnight, or at one, or at two, one is warm and energetic. At seven in the morning one has only to open an eye in order to shudder. It is not oneself but the climate that has changed. At midnight one is as comfortable as if one were in Italy. By the morning the North Pole has invaded the room, and one has become torpid or, as we foolishly call it, lazy. To rise in such circumstances would be an outrage on nature, like a bee flying round the garden on Christmas Day. That at least, I tell myself, is the reason why I do not get up when I am called in winter. There is probably an equally sound reason why I do not get up when I am called in summer. I may be able to think of it if summer comes.

XXVI. *Solitude*

I WISH I had a dictionary of quotations. I should like to turn up "Solitude" and see what has been written in praise of it. There is only one tag of the kind that I can remember. It is one of the few Latin sentences that I brought away with me from school—Cicero's (or someone else's) noble boast, "Nunquam minus solus quam cum solus." At least, it seemed noble to me when I was a schoolboy. It is, I suppose, some impulse to practise the budding wings of our ego that makes us delight at that age in the thought of solitude. Through solitude we become separate. We make a hero of Ishmael himself as a romantic figure, and half-envy the isolation even of the outcast and the misunderstood. May it not be that *Robinson Crusoe* owes a part of its popularity to the fact that it is a story of a lonely man? The eagle, the mountain peak, the desert island, all appeal to our sense of the distinction of solitude. Solitude—how charming a fancy to play with between meeting one friend and another! Where else but in this remote and secluded air shall we attain to poetry and philosophy?

At the same time, I do not like having dinner alone. How oppressively silent the flat seems with every one else away in the country! I sit down at

The Peal of Bells

the long table on which four candles shine round a bowl of oranges and apples. I do not suppose the table is really very long, but it seems to stretch before me away into the wastes of an infinite darkness. I get up and turn on the electric light for company. The mutton chop is done to a turn. That ought to console me. But what taste is there in a mutton chop when you sit down to it at a table surrounded by empty chairs? If there were even a dog or a cat in one of them, it would not be so bad. I would gladly share the mutton chop with a cat. I like this way of sprinkling some sort of green herbs over the potatoes. But the potatoes are not all that they should be. As I sit in the silence, in which no noise is audible but the occasional clinking of a knife or tablespoon, like the sound made by a ghost's chain in a haunted castle, I find myself thinking about potatoes and remembering old conversations on the subject—whether I liked them boiled in their jackets, the superiority of the skerry blue to all modern varieties, whether the use of sulphate of ammonia as a manure did not make them soapy, whether the proportion of soapy potatoes had not become greater in recent years. If only there were a farmer or a gardener or a gourmet or a greengrocer present, what good talk we might have about these things! When one is alone, however, the thoughts wander, and one's questions remain mere questions and fade away into the corners of the room unanswered. These beans, for instance! What is the secret of the

Solitude

French way of cooking "haricots verts"? Oil? Butter? These beans are excellently cooked, but, even in a French restaurant in London, they would—I should like to question the cook about it when she comes into the room, but she might think I was complaining. Better say nothing at all than be misunderstood. Silence. Silence and solitude. Wandering thoughts. Heavy pudding. I hope the cook won't mind if I eat very little of it. How long the evening seems as it lies stretched before me, with midnight an infinite number of hours away. I do not know what time it is, for the clock on the mantelpiece has stopped. That is the worst of living alone: there is nobody to wind the clock. My watch is at the watchmaker's. He says that there is nothing wrong with it except that the works are full of tobacco-dust. I wonder how tobacco-dust gets into the works of a watch. But I wonder in vain; there is nobody to tell me. I think I may as well go to a theatre. Not to a music-hall, for to sit alone in a music-hall depresses me. There is an "eat, drink and be merry for to-morrow we die" atmosphere about a music-hall that is endurable only in company. Besides, there is a play running at one of the theatres that I have been intending for a long time to see, because it is written by the son of my English professor of ever so many years ago. For the most part, my acquaintance with professors was involuntary and as casual as it lay in my power to make it; but this one

The Peal of Bells

I worshipped. He was a "character," a figure, with his white beard and his sea-blue eyes; and was a challenge to common men in every inch of his frame, from his wideawake hat, his nobly-thrown-back head, his bare throat, his velvet jacket, his red tie, down to his slow-moving feet. Had he been a revolutionist, he might have been a "crank" and have wearied us with windy nobilities. But he was a conservative, to whom the dreams of idealists were but a harmless illness of youth. When the Corporation passed a resolution that none of its employees should be paid less than a pound a week, he shook his head as over the beginning of the end of civilization. In everything but his dress he was a traditionalist. His creed might be summed up as a belief in the tradition of literature and the tradition of courtesy. He liked to speak of the great dead as one gentleman of another—of "Mr. Addison," "Mr. Burke," and "Mr. Pitt." Though I suspect he had been an idle schoolboy, he always spoke of his masters in retrospect as "my beloved schoolmasters." His courtesy, I am afraid, was not always answered with courtesy, for there were impatient young men in the class who believed that it was a professor's duty to help them to pass examinations, and who regarded digressions on Southwell and Miss Austen, on "sweetness and light" and "the tragic irony of things," as though their fees had been taken on false pretences. Hence occasional scenes, with stampings of feet and ironical cheers at

Solitude

the mention of some name outside the examination course such as Turgenev's. The class, indeed, though for the most part orderly enough (for he had a quelling presence), behaved so badly once or twice that, for the first time on record, he did not invite his students to his house to drink claret with him. "Gentlemen," he addressed us mournfully one day, when just before his appearance heavy substances had been hurled against the door of his private room, "you are not the sort of men I shall wish to know in later life." Yet I think there was no one who cared for literature who did not care doubly for it as a result of those digressions. As with flushed face he leaned over his desk and, nervously scribbling on it with a pencil, repeated a passage of great poetry, and ended in a hushed voice with the passionate asseveration, "Gentlemen, this is art!" absurd though it may seem, it was as though he had communicated a great secret to us. He was a man, indeed, whom it was possible to smile at as at a child, and at the same time to worship this side idolatry as a man of genius. To remember him is to cease for the moment to be alone. . . . I must go and see his son's play. What time does it begin?

When I arrive at Piccadilly Circus, I find that I am too early. Much too early. I have about three-quarters of an hour to get through. Where shall I go? What shall I do? If I go into the Café Royal, I may see somebody I know. But, then, it may be somebody I do not like. I stroll aimlessly along

The Peal of Bells

Shaftesbury Avenue, looking into the shop windows. I notice in one lighted window "smoked eels, 6s. 6d. per pound." Strange, I did not know anybody ate smoked eels. Stewed eels I had often seen advertised outside eating-houses in mean streets, and had turned from them with repulsion, but smoked eels are apparently a rich man's luxury. It is very dull walking about the streets, waiting for a play to begin. How melancholy some of the people look—especially those who are staring into the windows of the confectioners and the ham-and-beef shops. A pair of lovers are holding hands and looking into the window of one of the ham-and-beef shops, probably because it is easier to look into the window of a ham-and-beef shop than to find anything to say. Up Shaftesbury Avenue, down Charing Cross Road, and back through Leicester Square. Shall I go into Challis's buffet—just for old time's sake—to see if it is much changed? I remember that the man who was with me the last time I went into Challis's—it must be fifteen years ago—is dead. Ghosts, ghosts. I remember, too, the barmaid who served us—a tall, dark Dana-Gibson girl. I go in, but it is no use. Young fellows are drinking together. One of them is ordering something called "tonic water." This is not the Challis's I knew. I might as well be in a foreign country, of which I did not know the language.

It is still so early when I enter the upper circle of

Solitude

the theatre that comparatively few people have arrived. There is a vista of empty seats covered with faded red velvet. I cannot face such a wilderness, and I remain outside for a smoke. I see the bar is open. Someone to talk to perhaps. I haven't spoken to a mortal soul for hours, except a bus-conductor, and all we said to each other was "Piccadilly Circus," " 'k you," " 'k you." Standing beside a small glass of whisky, I decide to tell the barmaid that I knew the author's father. That should interest her. I tell her. "Fancy," she says, and goes on polishing the glasses. Long silence. I resolve to try her again with another topic. "Having good houses?" I ask her. "Pretty fair," she says, not looking at me, and then she begins humming a tune. It is borne in on me that I am not a conversationalist. Or, perhaps, the barmaid isn't. The theatre is by this time filling. It seems to me to be full of particularly miserable-looking people. All the people who have come alone, like myself, look as gloomy as owls, as if life disagreed with them. Others have come in parties of two or of four, and most of them look, to my eyes, empty-headed and silly. At least, those who laugh do. I realize for the first time how foolish a man and a woman look when they are laughing, and when you do not know what they are laughing at. At least, a man and a woman laughing in the dress circle look extraordinarily foolish from my seat in the upper circle. The man has a nose like a duck's bill and is an obvious ass. The woman is laughing a great deal as he talks. I try to believe that she is not really enjoying listening to him, but is laughing out of kindness. At last, the curtain rises. Soon we are all laughing. The play is a clever play, but, it seems to me, a little too contemptuous of human beings. These young writers—when they reach our age, perhaps they will be more tolerant. They will realize that human beings—— During the interval the man with the duck's bill seems to be surpassing himself in silliness. I would give half-a-crown to hear what he is saying. I am not sure that the woman is not as silly as he is. Still the play is a good one. It gets better and better, indeed. But I do wish that the author realized that human beings —well, after all, "in apprehension how like a god." I'm on Shakespeare's side.

The play over, there is nothing to do but go home. The fire is out, but I sit up for an hour reading a book of reminiscences, of which I do not believe a word. I go to bed, taking another book with me, *A Naturalist at the North Pole*. As I read, I admire, but am more puzzled than ever as to why any man who can live in London can go, even temporarily, to the North Pole. I should die, I tell myself, of loneliness. Those vast and empty spaces! And the monotony of it all! . . . After all, there is one thing about London. A man need never feel alone. There is always somewhere to go. Always some-

Solitude

thing to see. Always someone on whom you can drop in for a talk, if you are feeling in the mood for company. Seven million inhabitants—yes, that is something. Yawn, yawn. You may *have* the North Pole. Yawn, yawn. Give me London.

XXVII. *Farewell to Tobacco*

BOSWELL told Dr. Johnson that Steele published his *Christian Hero* "with the avowed purpose of obliging himself to lead a religious life." It is evidence of a touching faith in the power of the printed word that Steele should have thought that he had only to commit himself to a better life on paper in order to be forced into leading it for the rest of his days. Or, perhaps, he may have reasoned more subtly than this. He may have said to himself: "I will write such a book that, as the author, I shall be unable to fall from grace without exciting universal ridicule"; and, having failed to keep upright by any other means, he hoped to terrorize himself into doing so by creating a situation in which he could not slip without becoming the butt of every fool. The experiment, it is to be feared, was not a success, and for two centuries fools and wise men have smiled though without malice at stories of the Christian hero in his cups. "Steele, I believe," said Dr. Johnson, "practised the lighter vices." Steele himself, it is said, was bitterly offended by the way in which his fellow-officers subjected "the least levity" in his words or actions to criticism as being incongruous in the author of *The Christian Hero*. The publication of his treatise,

Farewell to Tobacco

evidently, brought him not the piety he hoped but the ridicule he feared. With such a warning from the past it seems madness in any writer who is not a saint to commit himself in public to a life of virtue. I have at times been timid of praising virtue even in other people lest I should afterwards seem a humbug measured by a standard that I had rallied to at least in words. And yet, like Steele, I am tempted at times to commit myself publicly—to commit myself publicly, say, to one of the lighter virtues so that I may know that I cannot become a backslider—strange word!—without also becoming an object of derision to my friends.

To-day, for example, I wish to give up tobacco. I do not mean that I wish to give it up as other men do, but to give it up finally. I have given it up as other men do again and again. I have trifled with abstinence for a lunar month at a time. If at the end of the month I yielded to temptation, however, I did not feel humiliated in the company of my fellow-mortals. I was merely amused, and regarded my lapse as a checkmate that must sooner or later have brought the game to an end. I am not sure that I did not even like myself a little better for having made a concession to the weakness of human nature. All men idealize themselves, and in the mirror of self-satisfaction weakness of will seems an unusually attractive form of good humour. I do not know how in the world men are ever to become virtuous if they remain so fatuously in love with themselves as they make it up with their sins. I should like to be able to say good-bye to tobacco in such a way that, if ever I reverted to it, I should feel so ashamed that I should have to leave Europe and begin life over again in the colonies under an assumed name. When I sat down to write this morning, it was in the hope that I might be able to utter a good-bye so terrible that tobacconists would grow pale when I walked past the doors of their shops. But how can I? Smoking, I am convinced, is for me a vice, because I cannot smoke without smoking to excess. But I cannot regard it as a vice in other people, so that it is difficult to denounce tobacco as a weed in the Devil's garden. If I could only hate it as Ruskin hated it, I might be able to write a new version of *The Christian Hero,* depicting a man who was too proud to smoke. But how can I hate tobacco when I think of all the pleasures with which it has been associated ever since I can remember? I grew up in the smell of it—pipe-smoke in my father's study and snuff in the nursery. My nurse was a good-natured Christian widow who every Saturday night went off in her jet-black bonnet and beaded cape to see her daughter, and who always brought back a little bag of pear or acid drops for me, and for herself a little bag of snuff shaped like the horn of plenty. She usually left the snuff on the corner of the mantelpiece, whence it overflowed, as it were, and permeated the room with the smell of a pleasant kind of pepper. How often have I sat

Farewell to Tobacco

on her knees, listening to the tale of the last agonies of the Protestant martyrs and sneezing where less fortunate children would have wept! How anyone can regard snuff-taking as a disgusting habit I have never since been able to understand. I associate it myself with the infinite kindness of a woman who would never admit that anything that I did was wrong and to whom I was so devoted that I remember arguing doggedly with my father that the correct pronunciation of "teaspoon" was "tayspun" and that "bread" should be pronounced "braid." It was with the smell of snuff in my infant nostrils that I first learned to admire a heroism that I have never been able to emulate, as I listened to stories of the relief of Kandahar and of the slave war in America (in both of which relatives of hers had taken part) and enjoyed at times the back-straightening happiness of having a soldier's medal pinned to my breast. It was in a cloud of snuff that I first heard of King William and the Battle of the Boyne and was inducted into music with "The Protestant Boys," "Dare to be a Daniel," "Ye Banks and Braes" and "Old Dog Tray." In later years, when I became a journalist, I tried to acquire a taste for snuff myself, for the printers in the case-room in Manchester were constantly holding out a hospitable snuff-box. On one occasion I even took to it as a means of giving up smoking, but a printer warned me that it was a still more enslaving habit. "I have seen myself," he said, "getting up out of bed in the middle of the night for a pinch of snuff." I suggested that at least it had not such a bad effect on the health as smoking. "I have seen," he replied, "a compositor falling on the floor in a fit in Manchester, and *he* was a great snuff-taker." It is lamentable that, just when you have at last discovered what seems a perfectly innocent habit, someone invariably comes along with a raven's warning. It is almost impossible to become virtuous, indeed, merely by changing one's vice.

As for smoking, how can anyone even regard it as a vice? It was only after years of thought about the matter that I was able to persuade myself that abstinence from tobacco was not a defect of manhood in a grown-up man. To have abolished tobacco would have seemed in my first years like banishing the clouds from the summer sky. There are two sights of which I never grew tired as a child—the sight of tobacco-smoke issuing from a man's mouth and the sight of a man shaving. How like Zeus in an arm-chair a man appears with those fragrant clouds about his head! How delightful it is in his absence for a child to take down his pipes and look at them—the crooked briar, and the long straight clay with the white hand embossed on the bowl—and to open the tobacco-jar and smell the most delicious of the herbs! Alas, it is impossible to admire such things for long without desiring to produce those magical clouds oneself and to taste the sweetness of that honeydew, as all tobacco seemed to be called in those days. I cannot have been more than

Farewell to Tobacco

five years old when, finding myself alone in the study, I made the great experiment. I remember, after a few minutes of it, creeping away to die in the hollow under the desk, flanked on each side by drawers full of sermons. I needed no sermons just then any more than the damned, and, indeed, I got none when I was discovered and carried gently to bed. There may be men who would have forsworn tobacco after such an experience, but, though I did not attempt a pipe again for a year or two, I was already a slave to the idea of smoking, and, even while I was still attending a dame's school, I used often to go into a spirit grocery on the way home and buy cinnamon cigarettes with another boy, which we smoked among the flower-beds and the glass frames in a nurseryman's garden. We frequently discussed whether it was wrong, for we both had consciences, but we decided without difficulty that, as cinnamon was not tobacco, to smoke cinnamon cigarettes was not smoking. "This is sappy good," the boy would say as he puffed at his cigarette. "Put your hand there"—and he would point to a waistcoat button—"and I'll show you the smoke coming out of my eyes." But, if you did what he said, he would suddenly bring the lighted end of his cigarette down on your hand, and two young smokers would find themselves tussling on the box-bordered path. I have heard of other boys smoking such things as tea and brown paper, but I remained faithful to cinnamon until I was old enough to smoke tobacco. Duke's Cameo cigarettes

The Peal of Bells

—you remember the little boxes, each containing the picture of a Parisian dancer or a statuette—are there any cigarettes like them nowadays? They had only one drawback: they left a smell of tobacco on the breath. I used, on reaching home after smoking them, to make stealthily for the pantry and to drink a large draught of milk, little though I liked it, in the hope that a smell of milk might deceive members of the family. I was convinced that the smell of cachous merely gave one away, and I had not the desperate courage of a fellow-schoolboy who used to chew the heads of matches and soap for the purpose of sparing his mother the knowledge that he was a smoker. What kind of drug-fiend she must have thought him, I cannot imagine; but it is a miracle that he did not die untimely of phossy-jaw. Even when we had taken to real tobacco, however, we did not at first smoke very much except during the holidays, and I should not describe myself as having been a regular smoker until the age of sixteen. By that time I smoked a pipe and one ounce of tobacco a week—Log Cabin or Pioneer or Tortoiseshell—which I always bought at the same shop from a very tall and beautifully dressed lady whose trembling slave I was. I thought she was like a Spaniard, for she had glorious black hair and glorious red lips and glorious white teeth when she smiled. I liked her to be alone in the shop when I went in. I always meant to talk to her. But somehow I never could say anything but "An ounce of Log Cabin, please,"

Farewell to Tobacco

and then "Thank you" as I took off my cap and went out. Thus I have also an association of love with tobacco. . . . But, if I were to tell you all the associations I have with tobacco, I should find myself writing an autobiography in ten volumes, for, save for a few brief periods of austerity, I have been smoking continuously ever since. That is why I am now so eager to say farewell to tobacco—to say such a farewell as will do no dishonour to a herb that has given me so much pleasure and at the same time will commit me to treating it with heartless indifference for the rest of my days. I doubt if Einstein himself could solve such a problem. All the same, I will try. Steep and difficult is the hill of virtue, and on the distant summit of it I descry the tiny figure of a man who does not smoke.

THE END

LIBRARY OF DAVIDSON COLLEGE

Books on regular loan may be checked out for **two weeks**. Books must be presented at the Circulation Desk in order to be renewed.

A fine of **five cents** a day is charged after date due.

Special books are subject to special regulations at the **discretion** of library staff.

JUN -7 1984